The Advaita Life Practice:

Balancing Relationships, Work &
Money in the Twenty-First Century

Jayant Kalawar

Action in Awareness™

www.advaitalifecoach.com
Balancing Your Internal Dynamics
For External Success

First Windsor Group LLC, West Windsor, New Jersey

i

The Advaita Life Practice

Library of Congress Control Number: 2012955436
ISBN: 978-0-615-73845-1

Contact Information:
First Windsor Group LLC
PO Box 614, Princeton Junction, NJ 08550
www.advaitalifecoach.com

Dedicated to Āiyee, my maternal grandmother

Ramabai Ganesh Betarbet (née Kaikini)
(1904-1978)

You nourished me and showed the way

The Advaita Life Practice

Table of Contents

The Advaita Life Practice

PREFACE

In publishing this first edition of **The Advaita Life Practice: Balancing Relationships, Work and Money in the Twenty-First Century**, I feel that a seedling brought out of the nursery of my own practice has been planted into public view, exposed to the sun, wind, rain and to bees, as well as, pests. The original seed was planted a long time ago, in the late 1950s, when I was but seven and eight years old. During this time, thanks to my maternal grandparents, I was able to have one-on-one *darshan* (the direct in-person spiritual teaching) of Baba Nityananda of Ganeshpuri more than once. In my early teens, I used to frequent *bhajan* gatherings in Mumbai with my grandmother, while my peers would be playing cricket. With her gentle guidance, introspection came to be second nature and the desire to strive for a subtle understanding of the life-experience was awakened in me.

Through these experiences, the Sanskrit terms for basic *Advaita* concepts also became familiar to me from an early age.

Fortune smiled on me for some inexplicable reason and I ended up in the prestigious Indian Institute of Technology (IIT), Kanpur. Here, I spent quite a bit of time reading and discussing Jiddu Krishnamurti, Ramana Maharishi and Sri Aurobindo with a handful of my class mates, thanks to whom I was exposed to a philosophical, yet practical perspective on Indian traditions. As was the case with most students at this institution, I ended up in the United States in the mid nineteen-seventies. From then on, for almost twenty years, the material experiencer was very much in the driver's seat.

It was in the early nineties, hit hard by a recession, that I turned back to introspection. I was fortunate to come across Swami Shantananda of Chinmaya Mission who had just moved from Taiwan to Langhorne, Pennsylvania. At the end of our first conversation, as I was struggling to bring up long submerged questions I had not ruminated upon since the seventies, he gave me a copy of Swami Chinmayananda's commentary on Adi Shankara's "Vivekchudamani." That gift began an introspective journey with the study and contemplation of the Bhagavad Gita and the ten major Upanishads. Live discourses, mostly during the early mornings in small groups led by the *Acharayas* of the Chinmaya Mission, provided the foundation for subsequently facilitating study groups of practitioners engaged in the study of *Advaita Vedanta*. One fellow practitioner was Vishwanath Murthy who became my interlocutor in challenging me to compare Adi Shankara, Sri Aurobindo and Ramana Maharishi. Vishwanath introduced me to Professor Frank Clooney, a Jesuit scholar focused on interpreting Indian traditions through lens of Christian theology.

My interaction with Professor Clooney, now Professor at the Harvard Divinity School, led to understanding how people outside Indian traditions perceive and attempt to engage with it. His perspective particularly provided an opportunity to reflect on questions raised by scholars like him, to further enrich and crystallize my understanding of the misnomers and mismatches that exist in how Christians and Hindus comprehend and translate Sanskrit terms; for instance, *deva* (translated as 'god'), *asura* (often translated as 'devil'), and *shraddhā* (translated as 'faith'), do not have the same meaning in Indian traditions as reflected in Christian theology.

Vishwanath also introduced me to Rajiv Malhotra of Infinity Foundation (and now author of "Being Different: An Indian Challenge to Western Universalism"), who introduced me to Professor S.N. Balagangadhara (Balu) of Ghent University and author of "The Heathen in His Blindness." A brief period of rather intense interactions with Rajiv and Balu, a decade ago, refined my perspective on how to engage in deconstructing postulates from major world traditions, and how current heuristics used on a daily basis by all of us arise out of syncretic interactions and conflicts among them.

The first impetus to write this book came following a talk I gave at a gathering of friends in January 2009. At the end of talk (reflected in the third essay in this compilation), the host suggested that I write a book giving my perspective on the Bhagavad Gita. Over the last three years I have been reading and contemplating on this work and finally put pen to paper in December 2011.The essays in this book, each based on a chapter of the Bhagavad Gita, have taken me to different points of inward exploration.

Cleo Kearns, my patient editor in this process of re-planting, is someone I want to especially acknowledge and thank for her developmental and editorial work on this book. Cleo's background in the study of religion and her work on the influence of India on American literature made editing this book into an engaged and fruitful process for both of us.

My wife, Kaveri, and my children, Anuva and Arjuna, have been very patient over this time.

Anuva, an artist and writer who also provided the illustration for the cover of this book, made time in her busy creative schedule to be especially encouraging through her curiosity to learn and with valuable feedback, as she incorporated the outlines of each essay into her own practice. This first edition would not have made its way into the public domain without the gentle prodding of Kaveri to meet deadlines and to be practical. Being an avid gardener, she is sensitive to seasons and cycles – the seedling metaphor I revisit in these essays comes from my enjoyment in watching her completely engrossed as she goes about her vegetable garden, talking to her seedlings and plants (and the rabbits, squirrels, robins, cardinals, black birds, the occasional blue jay and the rare goldfinch.)

Finally, I would like to acknowledge and thank all those who met in the study groups I facilitated over the last 20 years. Their questioning challenged me to deconstruct my categories and assumptions. I see each one of the study group members as an aspect of my Guru guiding me. Every time a question or challenge is posed or guidance is provided, it is one more manifestation of the *Guru Tatva*. I look forward to continual feedback from my readers and coaching clients even as I continue my own practice as a subtle striver.

Some of my readers will be unfamiliar with the terms in the essays. Meanings of several Sanskrit words, which are complex and subtle, are often learned by using them in practice with a teacher; during the **Advaita Life Coaching (ALC)** experience, they will become clearer and their precision and usefulness more apparent. In this book first-order meanings can often be derived from the context, and the glossary at the end of the book provides brief definitions for easy reference.

In my practice as **Advaita Life Coach**, when I am of help to people it is because of subtle energies of the universe. My hopes and intentions in my practice are expressed in this ancient verse:

Sarve Bhavantu Sukhinah | Sarve Santu Niramaya
Sarve Bhadrani Pashyantu | Ma Kaschid Dukkha Bhag Bhavet
Om Shanti Shanti Shantih

May All Be Happy | May All Be Healthy

May All Perceive Each Other As One Community | May

There Be No Sorrows

Om Peace, Peace, Peace

The Advaita Life Practice

| ONE |

A PROVOCATION:
We Cannot Balance Our Lives with Simplistic "Stress Reduction" and "Mall Yoga"

The Stage Setting | Relevance of Advaita Traditions in Twenty-First Century America | Actions without Attachments | Nature of Experience & Experiencer What Drives Human Actions | The Material and the Subtle | Possible Criticisms Integrating American Paradigms into Advaita Approach | A Provocation

The very process of living a joyful life in relation to relationships, work and money in the beginning of the twenty-first century requires robust physical, emotional, intellectual and spiritual health. It is a complex balancing act

> *What underlying assumption of material wellbeing do we subscribe to?*

that takes more than the simple techniques of stress reduction and a yoga class here and there. Rather, it requires continual awareness of our subtle nature. This book is a compilation of essays exploring how to draw on Advaita traditions to move towards this awareness and, therefore, to sustain a balance between relationships, career and finances.

The world we live in, at the start of the second decade of the twenty-first century, calls for maximizing material wellbeing. Across the globe, there is one underlying assumption that seems to be ubiquitous: we need to strive to decrease the apparent uncertainty of material experiences and to extend continuity of preferred experiences. The most common thinking that follows from this central assumption is that the only way we can decrease uncertainty and maintain preferred experiences is by acquiring and indulging in more material things.

I will make one provocative suggestion here: when you embark on understanding the teachings of the *Advaita* traditions, your thoughts about the current paradigm that calls for an ever-growing acquisition of material things will be subverted. The Bhagavad Gita for instance, which serves for many as a compendium text of these teachings, calls us to move away from a singular focus on the material and towards a balance between the material and the subtle. Even the process of becoming aware of one's breath as a very first step, when practiced in a persistent and sustained manner over a period of time, will give you peace and calm – but the probability of making that next million dollars will likely decrease as your focus changes.

The *Advaita* teachings are not narrowly focused on the strategic and practical; following them as **Advaita Life Coaching (ALC)** guides you is a matter of a way of life, and not a simple quick-fix for occasional problems of life. It is indeed a risky venture, to be undertaken only after contemplating all the pros and cons of the commitment in the context of your life goals. Many of us who start out on this journey may end up sticking to only some of the initial practices – something you can pick up in one of the hundreds of yoga classes that have sprung up around the world – in the hope that they will assist you in managing the stresses of living in the current paradigm of material acquisition, where success is defined as the size of one's dollar net-worth. For some practitioners it may indeed help in accomplishing just that. However, such a mall yoga approach has a low probability of taking us closer to becoming deeply aware of our subtle selves and truly balanced in our practical life in the world, which is the core goal of the *Advaita* practice and of **Advaita Life Coaching**.

The Old Paradigm | Holdover from the Twentieth Century

Today, a generation of twenty–something year-olds are asking questions that are vastly different from their parents; for the most part, they are not looking at acquiring houses or cars as

This stage reflects back a myriad of partially changing identities, continually fragmenting and churning our sense of self.

much as worrying about paying off student loans and making ends meet on income levels closer to minimum wage. They are increasingly coming to terms with moving back with their parents or living on incomes that do not match the expectations that were founded on a lifestyle provided by their parents.

At the same time, forty year olds with children are trying to figure out how to fund higher education while holding on to their jobs and homes. Baby boomers in their fifties to mid-sixties are unsure of when and how to retire.

At the back of our minds there is also the looming anxiety of global warming and depletion of natural resources like fossil fuels and, more immediately, how increases in energy prices will drive changes in the economy and in how we work, consume, live and relate to each other.

> *By observing our roles as performers we can enjoy the performance as it unfolds in the theater of our lives today.*

This is the backdrop against which we play out our roles on the global stage – a stage on which, in 2012, the media and leadership daily celebrate the communication revolution unfolding in hyper-drive, as large systems acquire information about every facet of our lives to store and repackage for endless redistribution. And, as we engage with it, this stage reflects back a myriad of partially changing identities, continually fragmenting and churning our sense of self.

It is against this background of uncertainty and the ups and downs in America today that I pose the question:

How can humans live a joyful life, given the material constraints, uncertainties and systematic challenges of the universe of experiences?

Defining Human Experience within the Modern Paradigm

A basic condition for playing out multiple roles on multiple stages in the theater of our experiences is to be in robust physical, emotional, intellectual and spiritual health. I call it **elemental health**, a manifestation of a balanced combination of the five basic elements experienced by humans: space, air, fire, water, earth.

The more robust the state of the elemental health, the better positioned is the individual to play in the universe of experiences. Today, for those gainfully participating in the structure built by the paradigm of modernity over the last few centuries, the practical universe of experiences consists of three major life spaces: relational (family and friends), work (service, professional or business), and financial (money). While the teachings from the Indian traditions are and have always been relevant in many times and places, ALC explores their application directly to the context as we live today in the first decades of the twenty-first century. ALC also explores how robust elemental health and the right attitude to the roles we play, regardless of the reception we get for them, are the keys to living joyfully. By observing our roles as performers, without anxiety and attachment, we can enjoy the performance as it unfolds in the theater of our lives.

Lessons of Enlightenment | What Drives Human Actions

Lest we think that this view is out-of-date or applies only to simpler cultures and times, let me clarify that the objective, rational approach of European Enlightenment with its powerful array of social, political and economic theories has greatly influenced my thinking and my experience growing up in India and, later, in the USA. I saw how groups of humans can indeed, as Enlightenment views of humanity theorize, struggle to reduce uncertainty and maximize continual and ongoing availability of preferred goods and services – provided that all subscribe to and are capable of the practices such theories tend to privilege. A running sub-theme contained in this book deals with the way in which the modern-self came to not simply follow those theories but also reflect them in its inner constitution, to see itself only as a rational actor with a goal to maximize material value. This inner change has set up contradictions within the rich range of selves that humans are, and part of the work of ALC is to explore other ways of seeing and understanding our self.

The combination of the "Arrow-Debreu Theorem" and the "Markowitz Model" provided the intellectual underpinnings for the global credit boom and bust that is haunting our lives today.

When I came to the United States in nineteen-seventy-five as a young MBA student, I was particularly enamored of economic theories developed in America, in the nineteen-fifties, based on the body of work of the eighteenth and nineteenth-century European intellectuals. These theories were focused on managing

8

and reducing uncertainty of complex events and making them applicable, in terms of contracts, between individual and groups of humans.

The experience of uncertainty in terms of time and space was to be managed to produce specific micro-physical experiences within a range of macro-physical experiences. The "Arrow-Debreu Theorem" led the way by providing a framework for a model to apply when goods are identified by when (time) they are to be delivered, where (space) they are to be delivered, and under what circumstances (macro-physical experience) they are to be delivered, as well as their intrinsic nature (specific, individual physical experience.) For instance, there would be a complete set of prices for contracts such as "1 ton of winter red wheat, delivered on January 3rd in Minneapolis, if there is a hurricane in Florida in December." The specifics of time and place thus mitigated the uncertainty of the weather.

This theory was used to generate the kinds of financial contracts with which most people are, at least, vaguely familiar: forwards, futures, options and derivatives, to name a few. On these contracts (and their breach) many a pension, mutual and hedge fund even now make their living.

Later, Professor Harry Markowitz developed a model for a best-case solution to the range of alternatives that people use to make decisions on a daily basis so that they have a better chance at getting more value for the dollars that they spend while, at the same time, reducing the chance of making a loss. Thus, the combination of the "Arrow-Debreu Theorem" and the "Markowitz Model" laid the groundwork for financial economics and its applications in resource allocation through investment banking, globally. Together, they provided the intellectual underpinnings for the global credit boom and bust that has haunted our markets and our lives since the nineteen-eighties.

A Provocation

Kenneth Arrow was awarded the Nobel Prize in Economic Sciences in nineteen-seventy two and Harry Markowitz was awarded the same honor in nineteen-ninety. In the second half of the twentieth-century, the promise of being able to manage uncertainty experienced by

> *The attitude of focus on material acquisition is a "Rājasic" tendency; the potential manifests to manage our space-time experiences for desired results in response to fears of loss.*

the mind through measurement of physical experiences and a planned set of structured physical actions was seductive. It meant that not only did humans not need to investigate any non-physical solution to their anxieties about well-being, but also that they could actively deny relevance of such non-physical experiences to their material lives. They were now in a position to control their destinies on a global scale.

By the nineties, having experienced three recessions and the challenges of raising children, I began to question the framework and the rules of financial economics that promised to manage uncertainty in our lives in this way. Having, in parallel, been raised in the

Indian tradition of *Advaita*, I began to use this alternate lens to understand the experiences and challenges in my life.

Twentieth Century American Paradigms IThe Advaita Perspective

An *Advaita* perspective encompasses and helps us frame and relate to the kinds of rationalistic, pragmatic and structured actions designed to reduce uncertainty with respect to the material world. To do this, we employ some categories in Sanskrit that draw attention to three

> *Advaita does not ask us to put aside the insights of economists and theorists of human behavior, with respect to the material world, but to understand them in a new way.*

different potentials or ways of characterizing human experiences and projects in the world. These categories are known as *Gunās,* and they are divided into the *Tāmasic,* the *Rājasic,* and the *Sāttvic.* The attitude of focus on material acquisition is a *rājasic* tendency. The *rājasic* potential manifests to manage human space-time experiences for desired results and as a response to fears of loss (the *tāmasic, sāttvic,* and all three *gunās* are discussed in more detail in the fourth essay of this book.) There is nothing "wrong" with a *rājasic* tendency. Indeed, some of the structured planning, risk management and monitoring techniques associated with this potential are included in the ALC coaching process; excelling at practicing these techniques, yet gradually moving away from undue attachment to their outcomes, are important steps towards becoming an advanced practitioner of **action-in-awareness**™.

The Advaita Perspective | A Personal Journey

The *Advaita* perspective regards classical economic views and enlightenment as valid on their own narrow terms but needing to be embedded in a much more comprehensive, self-aware, and acute understanding of our own nature and the realities around us. *Advaita* does not ask us to put aside the insights of the economists and theorists of human behavior, with respect to the material world, but to understand them in a new way.

My own journey began to confirm the usefulness of this reframing. *Advaita* sees the roles we play in the realm of physical and material experiences in terms of the concept of **Leela**, which means play or game in Sanskrit. The "player" in the game, the one who experiences its roles and dramas, is only an extension of the action in the game. In other words, 'that which experiences is an extension of that which it is experiencing.' I began to question whether the rules of financial economics and consumer psychology, which promised to manage uncertainty, were themselves a part of a certain play - the *leela* of active life in the material world - rather than an alternative and more rational approach to living. The first decade of twenty-first century experiences, of increasing uncertainty and challenges, together with a growing commitment to understand them through *Advaita* confirmed the limitations of classical economics and psychology and of the value of moving beyond them.

A Provocation

First, let me reiterate that the *Advaita* approach does not tell us to step away from this world of play, action and performance, especially if our role is tightly linked with roles of those to whom we find ourselves attached. On the contrary, it asks us to act out the roles very

> *Advaita Life Practice tools nurture and sustain the ability to move efficiently and with renewed vigor and pleasure between the various "leelas" or theaters of career, family, and finance.*

meticulously and even excel in performing them while observing the action without attachment to any particular aspect or result of the performance. Thus, excelling at actions without being attached to them or to their results becomes the key to a balanced life.

The sometimes surprising result of this attitude, when practiced diligently over a period of time, is a new ability to move efficiently and with renewed vigor and pleasure between the various *leelas* or "theaters" of career, family, and finance. A natural rhythm begins to arise and new energy is generated.

The Material and the Subtle

It was always clear to me, and it has become clearer over time, that a change in perspective that allows us to reframe twentieth-century classical economic and psychological ways of managing uncertainty through *What is the essential nature of the material experience?* the *Advaita* approach, which brings some immediate relief, cannot take place fully without a conscious and cultivated shift in perception from the material to the subtle.

As must already be evident, we will keep seeing the word "**subtle**" crop up again and again in these essays, usually in opposition to the word "material." The material-subtle opposition is, in many ways, better to understand than the more usually used material-spiritual for it does not suggest such a split in consciousness as the latter does. The subtle is not anti-material. It is a refocusing of how the material is experienced through the process of becoming aware of our nature as "experiencers."

We think we understand the material. It is something we can touch, smell, see, hear or taste. But what is the essential nature of the material experience? *Advaita* tradition states that the true quality of experience is *Sukshma*, subtle. Our experience of fresh lemonade, which is wet to touch, sweet-and-sour to taste, fragrant to smell, and cloudy to the eye, is subtle. Science tells us that a glass of fresh lemonade is made of molecules that are different configurations of atoms that are made up of charged particles. Quantum physics tells us that our physical tools experience the charged particles of the lemonade as manifestations of energy waves. When we give this experience a name, "lemonade," we make it into a gross object, an opaque, dense package of experiences, consequently losing our sense of the subtle.

The basis for our material experience is *sukshma* or subtle. It is the awareness of that subtlety to which *Advaita* points us. It is not that we leave the material behind. Rather, the understanding of the dynamic between the material and the subtle becomes the basis for the practices that bring us to detachment and efficiency in the *leela* of our lives.

Possible Criticisms

I would like to emphasize the difference between this subtle awareness, cultivated in and through *Advaita*,

> *Advaita Life Practice tools empower practitioners towards becoming better at performing actions consistent with the goals of greater joy, balance and efficiency.*

and any assertion of ultimate truth or dogma or particular religious belief. To re-emphasize, what I am describing in these essays is an internally consistent model of a process based on experience and not on *a priori* assumptions. This experiential model provides the basis for ALC practices to help with our journey towards a balanced life.

When I don my twenty-first century American hat, I become aware of two possible criticisms that may arise with respect to the *Advaita* approach. The first is that such an approach may simply lead us back to the dominance of magic and superstition over reason that the European Enlightenment worked so hard to overcome. The other is that it may lead to amorality or relativism, a challenge that has arisen from the Judeo-Christian perspective on the East, often expressed by my American friends, colleagues and business partners. The question frequently raised here is whether viewing the world as *leela*, with different roles to play at different times, makes for amoral selves. Let me briefly digress here, to put forth my answers to these objections, with the hope of helping concerned readers make a conscious choice of whether the *Advaita* path and the ALC practices will meet their concerns and goals.

Consistency with Reason: The ALC approach is based on an internally consistent, conceptual framework verifiable by practice and experience (this framework is laid out in the second essay of this book) which can be tested over time by evaluating, at periodic intervals, whether expected outcomes have been met. It is not a matter of accepting anything "on faith" except as a provisional stance to get started. The approach is examined, shaped and changed in practice and is

always open to question and reason. In fact
questioning, testing and reason were among the
greatest emphases of those who were my early
influences: Jiddu Krishnamurti and Ramana Maharshi,
among them.

Source of the Moral self: An ALC practice may appear
somewhat value neutral in terms of morality. It is based
upon a fundamental understanding of the human 'I'
ness formed through attachments to physical and
emotional experiences. Once this understanding of the
nature of the "I" has been established, the individual
client can make clearer and more detached judgments
about actions within the framework of his or her own
moral code. ALC practices empower practitioners to
become aware of what drives their current actions and,
by actions based in awareness, to move towards
becoming better at performing actions consistent with
the goals of greater joy, balance and efficiency for
themselves as individuals, their families and friends,
and for their immediate and broader communities.

How to Read this Book

What you see in this book is a result of twenty years of self-study through reading, contemplation and meditative practices of the Bhagavad Gita, the major Upanishads, Adi Shankara's "Atma Bodha" and "Vivekachudamani", "Avadhuta Gita", Patanjali's "Yoga Sutras", "Yoga Vashistha", Sri Aurobindo's writings, listening to *Advaita Vedanta* discourses by the *Swamis* of the Chinmaya Mission, and conducting year-round study groups with serious practitioners of *Advaita*. Admittedly, it is not "easy reading," and requires a lot from the reader to follow.

I suggest two ways to read this book of essays: anyone familiar with *Advaita* may want to read the table of contents for chapter titles and brief descriptions to scan chapters that may interest them specifically. This may give them a sense of what the book will cover. The essays can be read sequentially or in any combination. The reader with less familiarity of *Advaita* is most likely to benefit most from sequential reading of the chapters. For my coaching clients, I suggest a quick sequential read followed by a reading of specific sections, in their individually tailored coaching practice; the ALC practice also encourages contemplative writing in response to a specific question or questions that we jointly agree are relevant in the coaching conversations.

| TWO |

WHAT ARE YOU ACTING OUT?

Based on Chapter Thirteen of the Bhagavad Gita

The Theater and the Actor | Professional, Relational and Financial Spaces| The Stage upon which We Act | Towards Becoming Accomplished Actors | What Makes Us Stumble? | Getting Up and Going Again | Becoming Aware of the Mind | Making It in Practice.

This essay sets out the conceptual tools from the *Advaita* traditions which form the basis for the Advaita Life Coaching practices. It draws primarily on Chapter Thirteen of the Bhagavad Gita, titled "Yoga of the Field" (**Kshetra**) and the "Knower of the Field of Activity" (**Kshetrayagnyā**). This is an ambitious chapter in the Bhagavad Gita, based on the metaphor of life as play or theater,

> *What building blocks do we use to play out our roles in our work, relationships and money spaces?*

Leela, introduced in the previous essay. It succinctly describes the dynamic between the script, the stage, the roles, the actors in human experience, and the rationale for acting with them. It provides pointers on how to operate in this **field of knowing** and the rationale for doing so.

The first half of this Bhagavad Gita chapter takes a bottom-up approach to the conceptual framework on which its perspectives and recommendations for practice rests. It starts with our day-to-day mundane experiences and actions and links them to our mind. The second half of the chapter provides a top-down description of how the undifferentiated universal energy, *Brahman*, generates the basic elemental energies from which arise both the experience and the experiencer. Along the way, it begins to give us pointers of what a joyful state of living should look like, what causes the imbalances that take us away from the joyful state, and how we can overcome such imbalances to get us back on track. The building blocks described in this essay are used to find ways to construct and play out the roles for ourselves in our relationships, work, and money spaces.

Performing in the Relational, Work and Money Spaces

Let's start with an examination of the roles we play, as the Bhagavad Gita sees them, in the three fields of activities: in relationships, at work, and with money.

In the relational space we act out different roles, as we've learned them, in the fields of activity we are engaged in. For example, at home we play the role of a father or son, of a mother or daughter, of a husband or wife. I learnt what I have to do as a father from my father, my wife and, from trial and error, through the experience of fathering my children. In my role as a father, my family

> Who is it that acts out the roles? Who is the 'experiencer' in the process?

and my home are my fields of activity. The essence of "father-ness" and the model of how to be a father are now embedded in me. These experiences and internalizations give me the knowledge of the field of activity, the family, my role in the play and how to act in it.

When we examine the roles we play at work, as subordinates, colleagues to our peers, partners in a business, service providers to our customers, as bosses to those who report to us, we begin to see that we play multiple roles in this field of activity. In turn, each of these roles has its specific field of play and we learn the knowledge of how to act – as a doctor, nurse, lawyer, clerk, sales person engineer, analyst, manager, etc. - in that theater.

In the money space, too, we have roles to play which must be learned and mastered. For example, we play the role of how to earn an income, budget, save and invest wisely while understanding risks involved, to ensure what is available is used appropriately – now and in the future - for every member of the family.

By no means is the knowledge that one gains from the play or from our roles in the relational, work or money spaces final. In fact, the themes of the plays, the backdrops, and even the scripts of the roles we play are constantly changing and, consequently, we are constantly learning. As a parent, as our children grow, the activity in our role changes and we may find ourselves scrambling to learn that change. Change in our roles, in our play-spaces and in our

When we contemplate on the nature of the fields of our activity we will begin to answer the question 'who acts in them?'

knowledge about the plays, is a given. It is a reflection of the ever-changing ebb and flow of universal energy.

Who is the Actor of the Roles?

So, who is it that acts out the roles? Who learns what actions to perform in a role? Who is the experiencer in this process? Or, better yet, let us ask: "What is the nature of this experiencer, this actor, this learner?" It is through contemplation of these questions that we begin to access the subtle teachings of the Bhagavad Gita and the Upanishads.

The "Mundaka Upanishad" uses a powerful example to get us thinking about who we are. It asks us to picture a tree on which two birds are sitting: one is actively pecking and eating, and the other is simply gazing at the whole situation. When we act, we take the position of the eating bird; when we ask "who is it that eats?" we take the position of the observer bird. In actuality, we are always in both positions: as an actor or the eating bird and, as the one who observes the experiences and actions without getting involved, the observer bird.

The rest of this essay asks readers to put themselves in the position of the contemplative, observer bird, as the one that watches the actor bird eat the fruits on the tree of experience but does not partake in the experience itself. This observer position is called *Sākshi*.

When we begin observing and contemplating our roles, and the fields on which we play them, we can ask "what is the nature of the actor in our self in the various fields of activity we encounter?" Instead of answering this down–to-earth question directly, Sri Krishna, through the voice of the narrator of the Bhagavad Gita, gives us an indirect answer: When we comprehend the nature of our fields of activity we will, in the discovery process, begin to answer the question about *who* acts in them.

The Body as Our Primary Field of Activity

The first and overarching postulate in the thirteenth chapter of the Bhagavad Gita is that our body is our basic field of activity and that our "I" arises on this field. Our experience comes from the "I" interacting

> *The 'Aham' vibration is the actor, the physical body is the stage for the actions, and the 'Buddhi,' 'Chitta' and 'Manas' are the backdrop in the theater.*

with the operations of three subtle components of the human manifestation: **Chitta, Buddhi** and **Manas**.

In this postulate, the central actor is the 'I' vibration, represented in Sanskrit as **Aham** (I am) **kara** (that which does) and written as **Ahamkāra**. Often when transliterated into English, *aham* is lazily represented as ego. To reemphasize, *ahamkāra* is that which vibrates with the sound *'aham'* and comes closest to 'I am' in English.

The *aham* vibration comes out of *buddhi*, the capacity for awareness – the other two being *chitta* and *manas*. *Buddhi*, the awareness function, is an aspect of the subtle universe extended into the human manifestation. *Chitta* is connected with the physical senses and space-time experience, and captures and processes physical and space-time experiences into memories. It is the

The 'Ahamkāra' gains independent identity by associating with memories of physical experiences and distancing from the subtle, which is its true nature.

store-house of 'if-then' physical experience-based memories and includes the faculties of language and categorization. *Manas* is the lake of thoughts. The three - *buddhi*, *chitta* and *manas* - form the link between *Brahman*, the subtle universe, and human manifestation. The thoughts that occur in *manas* are produced as a combination of current physical experiences and the memories from *chitta* and, additionally, leavened by subtle wisdom from *buddhi*.

The *ahamkāra* or the 'I am' vibration which emanates in its pure form from the awareness component (the *buddhi*), at some point, begins playing a central role in attaching to the thoughts from *manas*. The *ahamkāra* begins attaching itself selectively to these thoughts, which are influenced by *chitta*, and through this selective attachment - what the west calls - the ego identity begins emerging.

The pure "I am" *aham* vibration together with the attached thoughts (a combination of memories from *chitta* and current physical experiences) triggers actions by the physical body. It is in this way that the *aham* vibration is the actor, the physical body is the stage for the actions, and the *buddhi*, *chitta* and *manas* become the backdrop in the theater.

> *While acting as the 'ahamkāra,' with attachment to memories of physical experiences, we are 'Samsarikas,' material experiencers.*

The *ahamkāra* gains apparent independent identity by associating with the memories of physical experiences and distancing from the subtle, which is its true nature. The process by which the *aham* vibration attaches itself to thoughts of physical experiences and categories, in the *manas* and the *chitta,* generates the scripts and the acting out of these scripts through the physical body.

To simplify further, let's ask the question: How do we go about playing our various and active roles in the three fields of action: work, money and relationships? Our answer will be: With our bodies, of course! To further elucidate this complex concept, let's use the currently popular Nintendo Wii Gaming system. The apparent field of activity is the screen, but what happens on the screen is based on the movements of the fingers of our hands and feet on the Wii device. This is no different from how we use our bodies to act out our social roles. The rest is just a projection. In fact, it is a huge projection on to multiple screens in a complex experiential universe with billions of people and animals and insects and plants playing the *leela* of the "Universal Wii," at the same time; a giant dynamic collage that is constantly being projected on multidimensional screens of which we only see three in all its kaleidoscopic beauty.

Once we accept the proposition that it is our body that is our field of activity, where we play out our roles, then the following question becomes relevant: "What constitutes this body that is our field of activity?" According to the Bhagavad Gita, the body in this framework is made of a subtle and a physical aspect. Our subtle body is comprised of five elemental states of matter and ten senses.

Before we deconstruct the ten senses that the Bhagavad Gita talks about, let us stop for a few minutes to contemplate *buddhi*, the function of subtle perception, again. *Buddhi* is the aspect of human manifestation with the most capacity to be aware of its own subtle nature, including its ability to produce the *aham* vibration. When we speak of being or becoming aware or of being the observer, we are talking about activating the *buddhi* function. Through such activation of the observer/self-awareness capacity in the *buddhi*, we can begin to shed attachments of the *ahamkāra* to various material and the not-so-subtle physical experiences and thoughts. In other words, while acting as the *ahamkāra* with attachment to memories of physical experiences we are **Samsarikas**, material experiencers. When the self-awareness aspect of the *buddhi* is continually activated we progress to becoming **Sādhakās**, subtle strivers.

Buddhi, however, is still limited. It does not include capacity to understand its ultimate source. That source is the extension of the undifferentiated universal energy, *Brahman*. ALC practices help a *samsarika*, the material experiencer, in becoming a *sādhakā*, a subtle striver. The journey of a *sādhakā* in becoming one with the *Brahman* only begins when the *samsarika* successfully becomes a *sādhakā*.

The process of becoming a *sādhakā*, a subtle-striver, is not a trivial one. It requires learning to:

a) Activate one's *buddhi* and, thus, bring its awareness capacity into play in our lives;

b) Use that awareness capacity to observe how *ahamkāra* plays with *chitta*, the storehouse of experiential memories, and *manas*, the lake of constantly changing thought vibrations triggered by physical experiences;

c) Observe how the *ahamkāra* responds and acts through the physical body;

d) Practice techniques to gradually detach the *ahamkāra* from attachments to memories and habits of responding to changing thoughts.

To return to the metaphor in the "Mundaka Upanishad," the observer bird, with guidance, begins to see that the consumer-eating bird has developed an ego, the *ahamkāra* 'I" vibration that has detached from the *buddhi*, the human manifestation that is a direct extension and connection to the **Brahman** or undifferentiated universal energy, and has attached itself selectively to structured memories in *chitta*.

Subtle Forms of Matter and the Human Manifestation from Our Point of View

The five elemental states of matter that are the source of the cognitive and action functions are earth, fire, water, air and space. These words refer not to the physical form that we

ALC suggests one way to begin contemplation is by reading a few paragraphs and stopping to process the content in silence, before moving on.

experience with our senses but to the subtle forms of

these elements. One way to differentiate them might be to call them five elemental energies: space energy, air energy, fire energy, water energy and earth energy. These constitute the functioning environment in the analytical framework we are considering.

Patanjali's "Yoga Sutras," reflecting the *Samkhya* philosophical framework, adds to this ten basic body functions divided into two groups: *Jnana* (cognitive) *Indriyas* (functions) or **Jnanendriyas** as a conjunction, and *Karma* (action) *Indriyas* (functions) or **Karmendriyas** as a conjunction. The body functions are set up in an input–output framework. The subtle physical sense inputs from the five senses into the body are processed by cognitive functions. The five *jnanendriyas* or the core human cognitive functions are hearing, touching, smelling, tasting and seeing. The five *karmendriyas* or the core human action functions are grasping, moving, eliminating, speaking, and reproducing. For each of us this is common knowledge, at least at the superficial level, because we continually process physical signals and act upon them.

We observe these ten basic body functions in play at any given moment. All our actions are some combination of two or more of these five output functions: for example, playing the violin is a combination of reading, hearing and moving functions. Together, the cognitive input (*jnanendriya*) and action output (*karmendriya*) functions are the core of the human manifestation.

Towards Becoming Accomplished Actors

How do the inputs get processed into outputs? The Bhagavad Gita gives us another pointer but, from here onwards, the level of subtlety increases rapidly requiring considerable contemplation to begin understanding the rest of the framework being presented.

The ALC process suggests that one way to begin such contemplation is by reading a few paragraphs and stopping, periodically, to process the content in silence before moving on. A second reading after the contemplative silence helps in putting the puzzle pieces together.

Building awareness of the subtle energies which trigger physical actions requires considerable inner work. We call work of this kind 'Sadhana.'

The analysis and categories presented forthwith are based on deep introspection. Their accuracy and usefulness are something you can experience by continually observing your own interior life.

The first step of developing awareness, of even such basic energies that trigger our ability to see or hear and to move, eat, digest and eliminate, is key in the *Advaita* view and requires contemplative, introspective practice. The approach is experiential, not text-book theoretical. Building awareness of the subtle energies which trigger physical actions, just as a small movement on the Wii console in our hand triggers

> When the 'ahamkāra' is merely a traffic cop, the system is said to be in balance, as being in the 'steady-state.'

major movement on the screen, requires considerable inner work. We call work of this kind **Sadhana**. This is where the **Advaita Life Coaching** process helps by suggesting tailored practices, and as a sounding board for contemplative questions, as they arise.

As an exercise to develop awareness, reflect on the grasping energy that we call hunger. The subtle energy of hunger (whether it is hunger for food, information or regurgitated memories) has a cycle of its own in our body. Over time, as we contemplate and become aware of it, we will notice how the grasping energy impacts cycles of energies that drive our physical sense inputs and action outputs. The ALC suggests structured meditative and journaling practices to assist in such self-contemplation.

So how do inputs get processed into outputs? Adi Shankara's "Nirvana Shatakam" (Six Verses to Nirvana) points to the input-to-output processing in terms of subtle centers in ourselves introduced earlier as: *manas* (mind, a lake of thoughts),

> *The creation of space-time and physical attachments-based identity leads to disconnect from our subtle nature. As the disconnect spreads like fast growing weeds, the potential for spiraling into imbalance increases.*

buddhi (the most subtle aspect of the human manifestation), *chitta* (detailed memory-based programmed instructions - e.g. if hot, don't touch), and *ahamkara*.

The *manas*, lake of thoughts, is a processing station where inputs come in from the five physical senses and are matched against memory-based programmed impressions to formulate an output response; the programmed output response is tested against meta-rules criteria and the *ahamkāra* directs it to the proper output function. For example, if the senses bring in information about a desirable delicious dessert, the programmed response may be "grab and eat it." The meta-rules test may fail the response based on the rule to wait until the hostess invites us to partake of the dessert. The *ahamkāra* holds us back to engage in small talk with another guest while keeping an eye out for the signal from the hostess.

When the *ahamkāra* is merely a traffic cop, doing its best to integrate the input and output signals, then the system is said to be in balance, also seen as being in the **"steady-state."** It is when the *ahamkāra* attaches itself to certain specific inputs, outputs and impressions in the memory (*chitta*), and overrules the detached awareness capability of the *buddhi* that the ego sense begins to rise. It is this dynamic of attachment that initiates an imbalance.

Now that we've alluded to a framework that can be used to understand the functioning of the human system and have briefly touched upon the steady-state functioning of the input-output processing, we move to the next set of questions: the first, "What makes a human system become imbalanced?"; the second, "What can we do to return it to the steady-state of balance?"

What Makes Us Stumble on the Stage?

What imbalances a human system? In response, the Bhagavad Gita makes it clear that it is not the environment that causes an imbalance in the human system. The changing nature of the five elements of the environment (earth, water, fire, air and space) is a given. The challenge is to function within the changing environment in a balanced manner. So the root cause of imbalance is in the unevenness of the input-output processing within the individual *buddhi-chitta-manas-ahamkāra* configuration, and not in the changing or challenging inputs from the environment.

Sometimes (for most of us, often) the *ahamkāra* gets trapped in the play of opposites, bringing in likes and dislikes based on attachment to past experiences and favoring certain experiences as pleasure and others as pain. It is then that the imbalances begin to take root and an apparently autonomous ego identity begins to form. This identity, which

What can one do to bring the human manifestation to a steady-state?

drives the imbalances, deepens through persistence in time and identification with material objects. The *ahamkāra* attaches itself to such thoughts as "I was or did such and such five years ago or, someone did such and such to me, and I like this and do not like that," and "I am a member of this or that household, city or country." Such persistence in time and co-location with space leads us to begin saying things like "I am a proud American from New Jersey." The creation of such space-time and physical attachments-based identity leads to disconnect from our subtle nature. As the disconnect spreads, like fast growing weeds, the potential for going into a spiral of imbalance increases.

This leads to the second question we posed: What can one do to bring the human manifestation back to a steady-state?

What Can We Do When We Stumble?

The response to this question – how we should act when we stumble in the theaters of our life – is also quite specific in the Bhagavad Gita: Humility tops the list, followed by actions that do not cause injury to our self and others, letting go of grudges and resentments and, above all, having self-control to not expend energies towards ensuring persistence of experience on transient physical pleasures. We are instructed to do so by being detached and even-minded about pleasure and pain and what is desirable and disliked. To achieve these behaviors, the Bhagavad Gita says, it is necessary to take a relatively introspective approach to life and focus on becoming aware of and discovering one's subtle nature. These straight forward criteria apply to all the roles we play in the myriad fields of activities we engage in: from being a daughter or son, to a parent, spouse, subordinate or boss, colleague, sibling or friend.

The Subtle Forms of Matter | Human Manifestation from the Point of View of Cosmology

Having sketched a bottom-up description of components that make up the human manifestation according to *Advaita* traditions, as represented in the Bhagavad Gita, we can now turn to a brief top-down description of how the human manifestation arises out of the undifferentiated universal energy.

The Bhagavad Gita describes a universal undifferentiated energy **Brahman** from which space, time and

> *The 'experiencer' is an extension of the experience functions that have abilities to process only the range of experience signals corresponding to that which it is made of.*

vibrations arise. Due to its desire to create and enjoy experiences, it becomes twofold: *Purusha*, the observer aspect, and *Prakriti*, the creative/active aspect. The creative property of *prakriti* is known as **Maya**. The sequence of how the universe of experiences evolves from the creative and active aspect, *prakriti* through its *maya* power, is described in terms that have been introduced earlier.

Adi Shankara, for instance, sees the evolution of our universe of experiences as follows: First, the subtle elements of space, air, fire, water and earth are created; each

> *The ALC process delves into the specifics of how our human actions functions are created so that the understanding and reflection of these details jump-starts the awareness process that leads to finding the steady-state of balance.*

element has three potentials, *gunās*, which we know as *sāttvic* (the potential to observe), *rājasic* (the potential to act in space-time), and *tāmasic* (the potential to act in the material here-and-now.) The *sāttvic* observer-potential of the five elements produces the subtle abilities to experience; the subtle ability to experience sound is born from the *sāttvic* potential of space, the ability to experience touch from air, the ability to experience visuals from fire, the ability to experience taste from water, and the ability to experience smell from the earth element. This is how the human physical senses are
46

formed.

According to Adi Shankara, the *buddhi, chitta, manas* and *ahamkāra* are created out of the interaction of these five experiential abilities of sound, touch, sight, taste, and smell.

The core functions of the human manifestation, the *buddhi, chitta, manas* and *ahamkara,* in this explication are actually an outgrowth, an adjunct to the experiential properties. They form a supporting, integrative platform for the five physical sense experiences. In this process, the experiencer is formed out of the experience functions that have the abilities to process only the range of experience signals corresponding to that which it is made of.

We delve into the specifics of how the human action-functions are created not as an exercise in mere theory, but that an understanding and reflection of these processes and details jump-starts the awareness process that leads to finding the steady-state of balance. The ALC process helps you deepen this awareness and contemplative process through guidance and by serving as a sounding board.

As a thought experiment, try contemplating on the *rājasic* potential. This space-time action potential of the five subtle elements produces the five action functions: the ability to trigger speech from space; the ability to trigger grasping from air; the ability to trigger movement in

The question now remains: how do we begin our individual journey back into balance?

space from fire; the ability to reproduce from water; and the ability to trigger elimination from earth. In turn, the action functions of speech, grasping, reproduction, movement and elimination, interact to produce the five vibrations which are the hooks into the physical body: **Prana** (the breath impulse), **Apana** (the impulse to eliminate, excrete), **Samana** (the grasping impulse to digest), **Udana** (the impulse to express, speech), and **Vyana** (the impulse to move).

In somewhat the same way, the *tāmasic* potential of the five subtle elements produces, through various combinations, the five physical sense organs of sight, hearing, taste, touch and smell, to support the subtle abilities of the cognitive functions and action functions provided by the five vibrations.

The components of the human system manifest from the five subtle elements of the creator aspect *prakriti*, itself an aspect of the undifferentiated universal energy *Brahman*. Here is a detailed breakdown:

1. The experiential functions of sight, sound, taste, touch and smell are functions produced out of combinations of the five subtle elements of space, air, fire, water and earth.

2. The experiential functions create the experiencer functions of *buddhi*, *chitta*, *manas* and *ahamkāra* so that the experiences may be enjoyed as play. The experiencer is, thus, an extension of the experience functions (this very important point will be referenced frequently in the ALC work.)

3. The action functions of speech, movement, grasping, reproduction and elimination are also produced from

the same five basic elements of space, air, fire, water and earth.

4. The physical organs of the sense of sight, sound, smell, touch and taste also come about from combinations of space, air, fire, water and earth.

5. The action functions are tied to the physical organs by the impulse energies which manifest as the impulse to breathe, eliminate, grasp, vocalize, think and move.

Making it in Practice | Journey Back to Balance in the Twenty-First Century

The question now remains: How do we begin our individual journey back into balance? For those interested, the 'how to' question is addressed in the Bhagavad Gita: With different practices of yoga, including *Jnana, Bhakti* and *Karma*. Each yoga practice provides a tested and proven map for the journey back to the steady-state of balance between the material and the subtle. The key is commitment to study, contemplation, and practice of the specific actions prescribed in them. Each requires dedication, combined with a burning desire to be on this journey.

The next set of essays will provide a perspective on the implications of the framework proposed in the Bhagavad Gita to understand ourselves more deeply, as we design and play roles with our body, both subtle and physical.

The Advaita Life Practice

| THREE |
GETTING TO KNOW YOUR ROLES & SCRIPTS
Based on Chapter Four of the Bhagavad Gita

Yoga of Knowledge | Performance: the Actor bird and the Observer bird on the tree of life. | The actor bird performs and the observer bird observes the performance | When the observer bird sleeps we perform, without reflection or knowledge, in ignorance.

In the previous essay, we discussed the conceptual framework of the *Advaita* traditions that we use in ALC practices. The framework describes how our actions in space-time are facilitated by internalizing physical experiences as structured information. Becoming aware of how physical experiences become structured memories, which

> *The Advaita approach helps us understand the questions: "What is knowledge?" and "Who is the knower of knowledge?"*

we then access to organize our actions, is a key step in the ALC approach to deepening the awareness required to bring us into balance at different times in our life-cycle. Such a process is described in Chapter Four of the Bhagavad Gita titled "Yoga of Knowledge." This chapter lays out the *Advaita* approach to reflecting on how meaning is formed from experience, and how that leads to forming a view of the universe of experiences based on categories;

The experiencer through physical senses creates memories. Memories are categorized in a structured manner, and chains of memories are reproduced as embedded thoughts in *chitta*. The lens we will develop to understand Chapter Four will consist of an understanding of

> *The process of gaining knowledge begins with giving names to the forms we experience followed by the inquiry of how these named forms interact with each other in our experience.*

"Knowledge" and "Knower-of-Knowledge;" from an Advaita approach it helps us understand the questions: "What is knowledge?" and "Who is the knower of knowledge?"

How does Experience become Knowledge for the Material Experiencer?

Experiences become knowledge when names are given to specific forms of physical experiences. Until we give names to specific experiences they remain undifferentiated, they are not knowledge. We begin to know our mother only when someone points her out and says "Mama" or "Mommy." When that association continues long enough, we begin to differentiate and associate that form of experience which feeds, cleans and coddles us, with the name "Mom." The memory of experiences associated with "Mom" are then accessed and used as knowledge when we come across the word as we grow up.

Another example of how we begin to gain knowledge is when we look up on a clear cloudless night and see shiny specs of lights from horizon to horizon. We experience this sight in awe and wonder. Someone tells us that the specs of light that blink are called stars, and those that do not are called planets, and the largest unblinking one is the moon. We are then told that certain clusters of stars have specific names. This naming begins a process of inquiry about the distance of the stars from the earth and between each other, and so on. In this manner, and through such inquiry, we generate knowledge about individual forms and how these named individual forms interact with each other.

We create connections between names and forms and begin to differentiate them when we inquire how these named forms interact with each other in our experience. This second step, of relating multiple named forms, gives rise to the knowledge of cause-and-effect. To extend the example of

> The 'Mundaka Upanishad' postulates two levels of knowers of knowledge and describes them as two birds, bound together, who live in the tree of knowledge. One eats the sweet fruit of the tree, while the other only observes.

"Mom," if the child breaks a piece of furniture and experiences an 'upset Mom,' this experience of 'upset Mom' gets linked to the 'breaking-of-furniture' experience. The cause-effect knowledge that is formed is: 'Mom-gets-upset experience follows furniture-breaking experience.' Thus, the universe of experiences becomes embedded in our memory as a chain of interconnected names of experienced forms. Spoken and written language provides the tools for such knowledge-creation and maintenance and also for understanding its limits. New words added to the lexicon (announced annually by the Oxford Dictionary of the English Language) are signals of apparently new experiences by human groups that are not reflected in their existing naming of forms.

Who is the Knower of Knowledge of Material Experiences?

Now that we have a sense of what "knowledge" means for the material experiencer, we will explore the questions: Who is the "knower" of this knowledge? What is the nature of that knower? As we have noted before, the "Mundaka Upanishad" postulates two levels of knowers of knowledge and describes them as two birds, bound together, who live in the tree of knowledge. One eats the sweet fruit of the tree while the other only observes. The eater of the sweet fruit is, in today's parlance, the consumer of experiences and specifically of those which have been given names. The observer watches the consumer bird but neither acts upon the observation nor has any attachment to it. The consumer of experiences, the eating bird, talks about "this is mine and that is not mine, I like this and I do not like this, I am happy and I am sad." The observer, the *Sākshi*, of experiences says very little and, when it does, it is merely to say "it is so and that is so."

The consumer of experiences attaches itself to the named experiences and begins identifying and defining itself in terms of the experiences it is consuming. So 'I live in a big house in London' becomes a part of our identity through the consumption of the experience of a named physical space "London" and a sub-set within London, "the big house." And, through such identification, 'I become happy or sad' depending on whether we can continue to consume that experience. If, for whatever reasons, the big house is taken away from us and we have to leave London our identity gets shattered. Now, we have to go about re-building our identity, by attaching ourselves to a new set of experiences. And, so on. The observer of the experiences that resides in us lives through all of this with nary a sigh.

According to Chapter Four of the Bhagavad Gita, the natural home of the observer bird is *buddhi* which is not attached to actions. When the observer aspect is activated,

> *How does the Observer aspect of 'buddhi,' which is innate in human manifestation, get activated?*

sustained and becomes dominant over the consumer self, actions performed do not result in attachments.

How does the observer aspect of *buddhi*, which is innate in human manifestation, get activated? The answer, in *Advaita*, is through a set of practices handed down from generation to generation – much like a mother teaching her daughter to ride a bike - and through practice, transmitting her innate sense of how to balance the body so that the bicycle glides. Like riding, it too becomes second nature.

Just as we learned to walk and run before learning to ride a bike, we must go step-by-step to reach a point where the awareness aspect of *buddhi* is activated through a set of practices. The first step in this process begins with observing and describing our relational, work and money spaces today, including the words we use in describing the spaces in which we play, the meanings we attribute to the words and the actions that result from the meanings. Do our actions support our goals? Which of the underlying meanings or descriptions of the spaces that we act in need to change? How did we attribute meaning to our memories and experience? How does the nature of meaning and meanings arise from our individual and social experiential memories? When we engage in this process of questioning and reflection, we begin visualizing the subtle energy underlying the experiences which give rise to memories, words and their meanings. It is in these visualized energy flows that we start becoming aware of the ones that drive physical sensations, space-time actions, desires and fears, and the ones that drive actions and the sense of awareness itself.

How Can ALC Help You Get Beyond Theories, Words and Categories?

The ALC process provides practices to help coaching clients through the assessment, contemplation and visualization steps outlined above. For example, we start by articulating your role in the work-space, followed by a short contemplative paragraph of the work-space. For instance, if you work in a biosciences

To progress towards excellence in actions, one has to act with minimal attachments. To act with minimal attachments, one has to activate the observer aspect and make it dominant over the consumer-self.

research lab (or an emergency room of a community hospital, an architectural firm, a bank, a school, or a community arts center), you could state your objectives in the short-run as: complete a series of experiments and write a paper based on those experiments. Your goal, in the long-run, may be to have a lab of your own to specifically focus on a certain aspect of research. How would you describe the field of biosciences? What makes it meaningful for you, besides providing you with a job? What makes your goals meaningful for you?

The ALC process for such contemplation, through visualization meditations, leads to clarity and reconstruction, not destruction, of meaning and actions in your work space.

Toward Excellence in Actions

In summary: To progress towards excellence in actions, one has to act with minimal attachments. To act with minimal attachments, one has to activate the observer aspect and make it dominant over the consumer-self that attaches to the experiences it consumes.

| FOUR |

HOW WE DELIVER OUR ACT:
IT'S THE GUNAS

Based on Chapter Fourteen of the Bhagavad Gita

The Three Gunās | We need them all | How much of each depends on our individual life-cycle | Becoming aware of our Gunās | Moralizing will not change our gunā balance.

In the contemplative practice of making the Observer, *Sākshi*, dominant requires an understanding of the building blocks that go into the making of the consumer-self, the *ahamkāra* with its entourage of attachments. The key building blocks of the *ahamkāra* are described in this and the subsequent essays.

First (and this needs to be emphasized), the play of all three potentials, 'sāttvic,' 'rājasic' and 'tāmasic,' are required in our human manifestation.

The first of these building blocks is an understanding of what, in *Advaita* traditions, are called the three **Gunās**, and described in the Bhagavad Gita as a way of understanding how the human manifestation is formed from the five elements. Each of the five constituent

63

elements of space energy, air energy, fire energy, water energy and earth energy has three associated potentials *Sāttvic, Rājasic* and *Tāmasic.* English translations of the Bhagavad Gita call *gunās* qualities. In my view, the more accurate translation of *gunās* is **potentials**. This

> *What constitutes the right balance of 'tamas', 'rajas' and 'sattva'-type activities for a harmonious life is contextual to points in our life-cycle and specific circumstances.*

essay, based on Chapter Fourteen of the Bhagavad Gita explores the role that the three *gunās* or potentials play, from the *Advaita* perspective, on the theater of experiences.

We Need All Three *Gunās*

First (and this needs to be emphasized), the play of all three potentials, *sāttvic, rājasic* and *tāmasic,* are required in our human manifestation. The combination of these potentials is required for balance and will differ at different junctures in one's life-cycle. There is, therefore, no implied judgmental or moral bias towards one or the other. Each has a role to play in the human manifestation. The *tāmasic* manifests as that which provides physical experience, here and now; the *rājasic* as the potential for action to achieve material objectives in space-time, and the *sāttvic* potential manifests as self-awareness.

Each of these *gunās* can manifest at either a higher or a lower frequency. At one extreme, *tamas* can manifest as obsession for physical pleasures, *rajas* as the ambitious 'I-am-the-doer' in space-time (thus accumulating tangible and intangible attachments), and *sattva* as the self-aware, overly passive observer of the actions carried out through activation of the *rājasic* and *tāmasic* potential. In the second essay we mention five elemental energies that come together in different combinations to form components of the human manifestation. Each of these elemental energies too, has the three *gunā* potentials embedded in them.

Thus, from an *Advaita* perspective, all humans have the three potentials – *tamas, rajas and sattva* – integral in their overall make-up. What constitutes the right balance of *tamas, rajas* and *sattva*-type activities for a harmonious life is contextual to points in our life-cycle and specific circumstances. For a child, the *tāmasic* activity of discovering physical sense experiences without the notion of space-time goals is appropriate. For a teen, inculcating goal-setting actions and becoming aware in a *sāttvic* way of imbalance-triggering consequences of certain *tāmasic* actions while learning to delay gratification to focus energies on the *rājasic* become more of a priority. As a general rule for a balanced life in the longer-term, the change in the combination of *tamas-rajas-sattva* is towards maximizing the *sattva* and minimizing *tamas* and *rajas*, as well.

How to Change the *Gunā* Balance

The human manifestation requires all three potentials to give rise to the experiencer. ALC contemplative practices help to activate the *gunā* potentials, to move them into a balance that is appropriate for a particular individual in a particular phase of their life-cycle. The *tāmasic* potential to experience the physical in the here-and-now, the *rājasic* potential of acting in space-time, and the *sāttvic* function of self-awareness, all need to be in play but in the right proportions.

Ingestion of food for the physical body needs the *tāmasic* quality of immediate gratification through taste and flavor, enabling the choice of foods. It also needs the grasping, *rājasic* energy of hunger and digestion for longer-term sustenance, and the *sāttvic* energy of self-awareness to know when we have eaten enough. However, an imbalance in the *tāmasic* could lead to a drive to eat sweet or spicy foods, in excess quantities, beyond the required response to the hunger energy. Similarly, the expression of physical human sexuality is driven by the subtle *rājasic* potential for reproduction but requires the *tāmasic* potential to be activated, through touch, taste, smell, sound and sight, for the physical body to cooperate and consummate (sexuality is one human expression that brings all five senses into play simultaneously, and the one reason, among many, why it is apparent often in our experiences and our expressions). Similarly, an imbalance between the *rājasic* and *tāmasic* aspects can lead to extremes of expression. If the *rājasic* is overly preponderant, sexuality can express itself through violence and control without the need for pleasure. If the *tāmasic* is preponderant, there can be excessive and draining physical

> In our emerging global culture, and in most of our lives, 'rajas' is highly predominant. That is why it is especially important to cultivate the 'sāttvic gunā' for balance in these times.

pleasure without addressing the reproductive or creative hunger.

When there is an imbalance in either the *tāmasic* or *rājasic gunās*, an increase in *sāttvic* energy is needed for two purposes: to simply maintain the health and functioning of the individual in the human manifestation, and as a "jumping off point" to achieve the goal of arousing the *buddhi*, the self-awareness that empowers the subtle striver to reach for higher states of being. In our emerging global culture, and in most of our lives, *rajas* is highly predominant. That is why it is especially important to cultivate the *sāttvic gunā* for balance in these times.

Moralizing Does Not Help Change the *Gunā* Balance

Moral strictures in attempts to balance *rājasic* and *tāmasic* potentials with more *sāttvic* ones are not effective. To illustrate, consider a moral ban on indulging in sexual expression other than for reproductive purposes. It may be based on a distant and dim social memory of the need to balance *rājasic* and *tāmasic* potential, but the moralizing dictum is solely driven by fear of painful consequences of hell. The process of how to bring the *tāmasic* to balance with the *rājasic* has been forgotten, and only the rule remains coupled with the articulation of fearful dire consequences. The articulation of the moral rule manifests as a social *rājasic* expression – "Do this because I, the Living Authority on Wisdom from the Past, Say so;" "Abstain from Pre-Marital Sex, because an Authority from the Past Said so"…and so on. Where there are procedures aligned with such moral restrictions of sexual expression, prayer and penitence for example, the moral objective is specified and the *ahamkāra* is expected to achieve the objective of celibacy.

69

Within the conceptual framework of *Advaita* traditions, we have to conclude that such an approach does not succeed. The *ahamkāra* is continually conflicted due to its range of attachments, including the attachment to achieving the moral objective of abstinence, on one hand, and sexual satisfaction, on the other. The moral approach does not offer a process to become self-aware

The ALC approach offers specific practices that lead to such balancing which, in turn, makes for behavior changes as a by-product.

of the *ahamkāra* and its nature. Nor does it offer one to moderate the attachments of the *ahamkāra* by bringing the observer, *sākshi* role of the *buddhi*, into play by rebalancing the three underlying qualities that drive different types of attachments. The moral dictum, whether it stands alone or when combined with prayer and penitence, provides the objective and a fearful consequence. It does not provide a contemplative process of awareness to re-balance the *tāmasic-rājasic-sāttvic* configuration, which would then reflect in changed behavior patterns, as a result.

In contrast, the **Advaita Life Coaching** approach offers specific practices that lead to such balancing which, in turn, makes for behavior changes as a by-product. This gives an additional

> *Where do you fall in the range of the 'gunā' mix between one-hundred percent 'sāttvic' and one-hundred percent 'tāmasic'?*

perspective to the moral-amoral discussion which we briefly touched upon in the first essay. The ALC perspective does not absolve individuals from following rules laid down in a particular human group. It is also not a perspective on how social laws should be developed or whether moral rules should or should not be espoused. That would require unfolding of a different discussion from *Advaita* perspective and, potentially, a different book. What the ALC interpretation of *Advaita* traditions does underscore is that change in humans is achieved through deepening of self-awareness with focus on achieving and sustaining a balance between the three *gunās*.

What is My *Gunā* Composition?

One of the questions that those approaching ALC practices may raise is: Where do I fall in the range of the *gunā* configuration, between one-hundred percent *sāttvic* and one-hundred percent *tāmasic*? And, this may trigger an existential angst about one's self-worth. Let's put them into context once again: *gunās* are postulated in *Advaita* as potential for three types of actions

There are no cookie cutter processes or outcomes in the ALC process. The mix of breath work, contemplation, meditation, planning and monitoring tools suggested are individualized.

embedded in each the essential elements of space energy, air energy, fire energy, water energy and earth energy. The mix and match of these elements produces human components with a combination of the potentials leading to a range of awareness-observer behaviors (*sāttvic*), space-time material acquisition goal-based actions (*rājasic*), and physical sense-experience based actions (*tāmasic*).

In twenty-first century terms, we may differ in how we describe essential elements and how they combine to form human components. Water as H_2O and air as O_2 are now known to form a substantial part of the human body and impact its maintenance, for example. The broad process of how the combination of elements leads to the human manifestation and sustenance is the same. What is different in the *Advaita* perspective is that the elements themselves already have embedded in them the three potentials of *tamas, rajas* and *sattva* which lead to different types of human activities. It is this construct from *Advaita* that leads to the development of ALC practices of working with the elements of wind, fire, earth, air and space for rebalancing. You will gain a better understand of this when you begin to work with our array of concrete practices that help balance the *gunās* on your path.

No Cookie Cutter Solutions to Balancing *Gunās*

In the ALC process, we begin our first interaction with coaching clients with a simple non-judgmental measure of where they are in the work, relational and money spaces, and where they would like to get to. If the individual is quite satisfied about where they are situated currently, the ALC process may be redundant for them in this particular point of their life-cycle. At different times in the individual life-cycle, the combinations of the three *gunās* required for balance differs. For adults in or entering the work, relationships and financial spaces of the twenty-first century, and for whom the ALC process is best designed to help, balancing the three *gunās* is a process collaboratively tailored to a specific situation by the ALC coach and the client.

There are no cookie cutter processes or outcomes in the ALC process. A twenty-eight year old may seek to reach a balance through a commitment in the relational space, while a forty-five year old may look towards improving balance by deepening career commitments in the professional space. The mix of awareness, planning and monitoring tools that would be suggested for use are individualized.

Recap: What Role do *Gunās* Play in a Balanced Life?

The question that should follow is: What role do *gunās* play in helping reaching and maintaining a balanced life? One way of relating to this is by using the metaphor of gears in a car: the first and second gears come into use to get the car moving from a standstill or on an uphill incline; the fourth gear and over-drive are effective when the car is cruising at higher speeds.

Similarly, *tāmasic* actions are required by the physical body to

> *The typical week day of an adult in the twenty-first century city or suburb is similar to going on a hunt, albeit with different forms of 'prey' and, therefore, different set of tools to use.*

carry out its functions of safety (the unconscious reaction of the body to touching a hot surface is a *tāmasic* act); the process of hunting, including observing a flight of birds, fashioning appropriate hunting tools, planning and executing a hunt, brings *rājasic* qualities into action; contemplation at the end of day, to reflect on and become aware of how we used our body and mind hunt successfully hunt keeping physical safety in mind, brings *sāttvic* potential into play.

The typical week day of an adult in the twenty-first century city or suburb is similar to going on a hunt, albeit with different forms of 'prey' (in the sense of objectives to meet) and, therefore, different set of tools to use. Ensuring safety while commuting and having a hunger-satisfying morning coffee and breakfast requires a mix of the *tāmasic* (pleasurable tastes like hot, sweet and fat) and *rājasic* (the "got to get to work in the next thirty minutes, so eat and drink coffee while driving" impetus.) The kind of breakfast to have - from a longer term healthful perspective - requires bringing in *sāttvic* awareness of the choices and their impact on the complex *tāmasic* and *rājasic* actions, into play.

One can argue that hot, sweet and fatty was exactly the kind of food the human body required in the centuries past when we were physically more active and food was not always available in plentiful. The body, therefore, continues to act the same way as it has been programmed. That is the point here: acting at a physical level, based on prior programming without setting objectives, is *tāmasic*. Setting objectives of a balanced diet, in the current environment of low physical activity and availability of nutrition, and acting to achieve them is *rājasic*. Being able to observe the changed situation from centuries ago and spur action to move from being *tāmasic* to *rājasic*, is *sāttvic*.

Recognizing the Three *Gunās* in Action

How does someone who has a predominant *sāttvic*, *rājasic* or *tāmasic* temperament act and how can they be identified? Again, we need to keep in mind that such individuals with a predominant temperament may be in balance at a given moment of time, given a wider perspective on their lives. Predominance of any one of the three potentials does not imply imbalance.

A *sāttvic* individual will engage in minimal activities that consume sensual pleasures, and will also not have longer-term planned activities to achieve material objectives. As an example of a *sāttvic* role, Gautama Buddha evolved the concept of a **Bhikku**. He or she not only eats minimally, often by begging for food once a day, sleeps in the open, has minimal clothes, and spends time in sitting meditation, and is available and open to anyone approaching him or her for conversation. None of these requires actions beyond the minimal. In the context of the twenty-first century, such an individual with a predominantly *sāttvic* expression may be easily mistaken for a homeless panhandler.

A predominantly 'rājasic' person can easily be most easily identified today. Professions or work that require meeting material objectives effectively in a timely manner – tap into the reservoir of 'rājasic' potential.

The *bhikku's* capability to be in this *sāttvic* state for a sustained period is an outcome of contemplative and meditative practices to become aware of one's attachments and then act to overcome them. This is a capacity of *buddhi*, one of our basic components of a human manifestation (which are *ahamkāra, buddhi, chitta* and *manas.*) It is ideally not an objective achieved through the *ahamkāra's* sacrifice of material desires through determination and endurance, which would be a *rājasic* move, or through renouncing physical pleasures, which would be a *tāmasic* one. Western-oriented seekers often make a mistake here by substituting a will-driven, *rājasic* asceticism for a genuine attainment of a *sāttvic*-state achieved, not through *rājasic* push, but through cultivation of *buddhi*. The distinction is subtle but important and an example of why subtlety of the kind *Advaita* offers can be so useful in **Sadhana**.

A predominantly *rājasic* person can easily be identified today. Entrepreneurs, businesspersons, nurses, doctors, journalists, teachers, lawyers, engineers, and associates at a fast food outlet – professions or work that require meeting material objectives effectively in a timely manner – tap deeply into the reservoir of *rājasic* potential. On one hand, such individuals are known to be willing and able to forego immediate sensual pleasures or, at least, defer them, for example, holding off until the end of the week to bring *tāmasic* functions into play to enjoy a six-pack or bottle of wine. On the other hand, their *rājasic* focus on professional and financial objectives can also make them oblivious to the balance required in the relational space. Steve Jobs, as his biographer presents him, seems typical of a predominantly *rājasic* entrepreneur who was able to achieve the material objective of creating great products and financial success and also displayed an apparent obliviousness in the relational space. For most of us, underplaying the importance of the *sāttvic* functionality in our work, relationships and money spaces may create more than a desired imbalance. However, we should also note that someone like a Steve Jobs may be quite content with the apparent imbalance of achieving success in the work and money space with a concomitant underachievement in the relational space, just like the accomplished *bhikku* who is content living in a manner that predominantly brings the *sāttvic* potential into play that, as a by-product, underplays the *rājasic* and *tāmasic* potentials.

Someone who looks for ways of making just enough money to satisfy her basic needs and sensual pleasures on a day-to-day basis, does not make long-term commitments in the relational space, nor is interested in achievements in business, professional or work areas, has predominantly *tāmasic* quality. The beloved character of "The Dude" in the famous Coen brothers' film "The Big Lebowski" is such a *tāmasic* type and part of our pleasure in watching him is in seeing that role played out so consistently. Again, such a person may be quite content with this mode of living of a life and express that he or she is in balance.

| FIVE |

HOW WE ACT OUT OUR DESIRES & FEARS
Based on Chapter Sixteen of the Bhagavad Gita

*Samsarika, the Material Experiencer | Sādhakā, the Subtle Striver |
Exhortations Do Not Work*

Chapter Sixteen of the Bhagavad Gita is down-to-earth
compared to the other chapters and provides an
opportunity to explore how the concepts of the four
cognitive functions (*jnānendriyās*), five action functions
(*karmaendriyās*), and the three potentials (*gunās*), apply
to our worldly
experiences. It does so by

> *What are the attributes of a
> 'Sādhakā,' the Subtle Striver?*

differentiating the
characteristics of the *Samsārikā* - material experiencer –
the one who is more attuned to keep doing the rounds
of the material world, and the *Sādhakā* – the one who is
likely to succeed in going towards the subtle.

Samsārikā, the Material Experiencer | *Sādhakā*, the Subtle Striver

Chapter Sixteen begins with a brief description of how one can recognize the subtle striver, the *sādhakā*, and then focuses on the characteristics of the *samsarika*, the material experiencer. The qualities describing a subtle striver should not to be undertaken as a list of objectives to be achieved, but more like a set of by-product expressions that evolve naturally as the striver proceeds in her or his *sadhana*. Fearlessness, purity of temperament, steadfastness in pursuit of *jnana* subtle knowledge, self-control, absence of greed, gentleness, freedom from restlessness, and absence of envy or pride, are only a partial list of attributes that a subtle striver displays with increasing clarity as the *sadhana* becomes firmly established in the striver's daily routine.

Setting up qualities such as gentleness or absence of greed as a goal to be achieved by sheer force of will not only does not make for a subtle striver, it is also counterproductive. Attempting to change one's *gunā* composition using will power ("I want to become more *sāttvic* and less *tāmasic*") makes you a doer, an actor fully involved in the achievement process, replete with resulting attachments and weakened observer function. It should come as no surprise that exhortations of "do not be greedy" or "be fearless" or "be gentle" do not produce expected results and only lead to confused posturing and pretensions. It is the core practices of study, contemplation and meditation that lead to flowering of the qualities of the subtle striver described here. The objective is to undertake the practice in a structured and disciplined manner – the steps in the practices are the objective in itself. The characteristics of the *sādhakā*, the subtle striver, are by-products of the practices.

We are All Material Experiencers and Subtle Strivers

Humans are complex creatures and, as mentioned earlier, we try to understand ourselves to the extent that language permits, by using various categories of description. We are rich, poor, tall, short, white, brown, black, brown-eyed, and blue-eyed. We are kind,

aggressive, extroverted or introverted; the list goes on.

Using such categories and labels helps create a cognitive lens to interact with the

> *The use of categories and labels reflects an implicit underlying model we have embraced, even though we may not consciously articulate the model or even accept that we operate within its terms.*

world of our experiences. The use of such categories

reflects an implicit underlying model we have

embraced, even though we may not consciously

articulate the model or even accept that we operate

within its terms. The model is the lens through which

we see the world. Even here, where we are trying to

free ourselves from attachment to such categories, we

still have to employ them in the process. The three

gunās are just such a "lens." Some lenses are more

useful than others, though all are partial. Using the lens

of the three *gunās* has been found very useful over

many centuries of practice, observation and self-

reflection. The Advaita Life Coaching model is based

on the Bhagavad Gita. We have already introduced

some of the basic terms of that model. Let us look at them again here.

Drivers of the core model of human manifestation in the Bhagavad Gita are:

a) The physical senses

b) *Chitta*: structured memories of past actions arising as thoughts

c) *Buddhi*: capacity for self-awareness

d) *Ahamkāra*: that arises out of *buddhi's* capacity for awareness but begins to use that capacity to mis-identify itself with experiences stored in *chitta*

e) *Manas*: the lake of thoughts, which is a live stage for interaction between the three functions described above.

Three types of human behaviors that arise out of this core model are categorized as:

a) *Tāmasic* type: immediate gratification

b) *Rājasic* type: delaying gratification through play in space-time

c) *Sāttvic* type: observing but not acting

The task is not to rid ourselves of the characteristics belonging to these categories, but to move towards being an observer of the roles, scripts and fields of play on which we act them out. *Samsārikās* or material experiencers who become aware of their complex nature, using their *buddhi* capacity of self-awareness, tend to exhibit behaviors of *sādhakās* or subtle strivers. They are said to have **Deva Gunā** or awareness potential, from the root word **Divya** or light of awareness (here, again, the frequent English translation of *deva* to "god" within the framework of Christian theology is highly misleading.)

Chapter Sixteen of the Bhagavad Gita offers a long list of characteristics typical of such *devas*, subtle strivers: fearlessness, purity of temperament, steadfastness in the "Yoga of Knowledge," giving, self-control, sacrifice, the study of wisdom texts, a burning desire to

88

understand one's own nature, candor and straightforwardness, harmlessness, truth, absence of wrath, self-denial, calm, absence of fault-finding, compassion to all beings, absence of greed, gentleness, modesty, freedom from restlessness, energy, forgiveness, patience, cleanness, and absence of envy and pride.

The chapter then turns its gaze on to the other side of the coin, on the material experiencers, the *samsārikās*, who seek immediate or delayed material gratification. These are the **Asuras** – from the root word **Sura** or one who is learned and wise, making A-*Sura*, the one who is not wise; again, the usual translation in the West of *asura* as "devil", while it fits into Christian theological constructs, is misleading. *Asuric* characteristics are pride, arrogance, excessive self-esteem, wrath, harshness and ignorance.

Each one of us experiences these on a daily basis as natural human traits in ourselves and others – in some more than others. The behaviors that result are also familiar to us. They are described succinctly in Chapter Sixteen of the Bhagavad Gita: "Bound by a hundred bonds, devoured by wrath and lust, unweariedly occupied in amassing unjust gains which may serve their enjoyment and the satisfaction of their craving, always they think: "To-day I have gained this object of desire, to-morrow I shall have that other; to-day I have so much wealth, more I will get to-morrow. I have killed this my enemy, the rest too I will kill. I am a lord and king of men, I am perfect, accomplished, strong, happy, fortunate, a privileged enjoyer of the world; I am wealthy, I am of high birth; who is there like unto me? I will sacrifice, I will give, I will enjoy."

(Chapter 16, verses 12 -13, trans. Sri Aurobindo)

Billionaire-philanthropists in the twenty-first century do sacrifice somewhat so they can gain more. They do give and get fame and adulation. And they enjoy it, as well. How do they come to be privileged enjoyers? Sri Aurobindo's translation of the pithy verses of the Gita above says it succinctly.

What Makes for the Material Experiencer in the Twenty-First Century?

The twenty-first century paradigm of the global flow of capital, with the concomitant need to assert power, leads to scripts we play out every day on the world stage (that are also beamed

> *We are convinced that to be who we think we are - our core identity - we need a delicious meal, a house, a car, a bicycle, a degree in law, medicine, business or engineering, and a wardrobe that changes with the seasons fashions.*

into our homes, work, schools) that encourages the development of the *asuric* identity and the dominance of the *samsarika* in its systems. All of us are an integral part of this play, working in collusion to allow this tremendous cultural emphasis on being wrathful, harsh and ready to do anything for material gains.

Let's risk over-simplification, to begin with, and consider a two-step process that leads from gratification-focused actions (whether immediate or delayed) to a miserable, unhappy situation. The first step is that we identify ourselves with the objects of our physical experience by forming attachments to them. We are convinced that to be who we think we are - our core identity - we need a delicious high-calorie meal, a house, a car, a bicycle, a degree in law, medicine, business or engineering, and a wardrobe that changes with the seasons fashions. We, then, desire to obtain and retain those objects to which we form attachments.

The second step is triggered when we cannot meet or exceed the demands of our desires for such objects, a goal which is unreachable given their infinite expansion and repetition. Not meeting desires leads to resentment, which bubbles up as anger. Anger disables access to the self-awareness capacity of *buddhi* that keeps us in balance in the mental plane, leading to impulsive, destructive, violent behaviors. This ladder of fall is described elegantly in Chapter Two Verses 62-67 of the Bhagavad Gita (Trans. Sri Aurobindo):

> *In the Advaita Life Coaching approach, an examination of where we are on the 'Samsārikā-Sādhakā' range becomes an integral part of the process.*

62. In him whose mind dwells on the objects of sense with absorbing interest, attachment to them is formed; from attachment arises desire; from desire anger comes forth.

63. Anger leads to bewilderment, from bewilderment comes loss of memory; and by that the intelligence is destroyed; from destruction of intelligence he perishes.

64-65. It is by ranging over the objects with the senses, but with senses subject to the self, freed from liking and disliking, that one gets into a large and sweet clearness of soul and temperament in which passion and grief find no place; the intelligence of such a man is rapidly established (in its proper seat).

66. For one who is not in Yoga, there is no intelligence, no concentration of thought; for him without concentration there is no peace, and for the unpeaceful how can there be happiness?

67. Such of the roving senses as the mind follows, that carries away the understanding, just as the winds carry away a ship on the sea.

How to Become More of a Subtle Striver, the *Sādhakā*

The Bhagavad Gita not only details the steps on the "way down" to the *asuric-samsaric* level but also the way to re-emerge from the fall. Based on its experiential model, we see described the process by which the *asura* tendencies are brought forth in *samsarikas* and how we can reemerge from the fall as *sādhakās*, subtle strivers.

In the Advaita Life Coaching approach, an examination of where you are on the *samsarika-sādhakā* range becomes an integral part of the process. We do not do this to grade or beat up on ourselves, or to moralize. The basic motivator for such self-examination has to come from recognizing that you are out of balance and unhappy and, therefore, need to begin an exploration. There has to be a motivation to get back to a balanced and harmonious life, to a place where you can observe and expertly surf upon the agitations that come and go as waves, without identifying with or getting attached to them.

The Take Away

Changing the way we do things and how we make the change happen comes when we exercise *buddhi*, our capacity for self-awareness, a process we learn through experience and, to some extent, by drawing upon the experiences of those who have "been there, done that." The latter is more easily said than done. Someone may say we could emulate the Gautama Buddha by giving up desires and living a simple life. However, this advice is an abstract guidance that does not help us to either activate or exercise our *buddhi*. Until we understand, through practice and experience, the complexity involved in giving up desires, and what it entails, the prescription to simplify one's life will be difficult to "take."

The ALC process helps you to develop practices that are most suitable for you at a given time in your life cycle, to enable you to activate your *buddhi* capacity for self-awareness. As you continue to practice contemplation and meditation, small realizations begin dawning about the dynamic of what leads to attachments and desires, anger and frustration, and destructive actions. Realization of the specific dynamics within you is a reflection of exercising your *buddhi* self-awareness that you can draw upon rest of your life.

The next three essays focus on specific practices in the self-examination process to move us towards becoming more of a *sākshi*, an observer.

SIX

CHALLENGE OF MOVING TOWARDS ACTION WITHOUT ATTACHMENT

Based on Chapter Seventeen of the Bhagavad Gita

Passionate Commitment | Shraddhā| Shraddhā through the Three Gunās |Four Types of Actions | Āhārā, Grasping and Consuming | Yagnyā, Setting up Environment for Subsequent Actions | Tapasyā, Delaying Gratification through Focused Action | Dāna, Giving Away Fruits Obtained through Tapasyā

In this essay, based on Chapter Seventeen of the Bhagavad Gita, we will understand the crucial the role of *Shraddhā* - passionate commitment - to the process of becoming a subtle striver, and the importance of the concept of the four action types, or the modes of action, through which we work and operate in our human manifestation.

The Importance of *Shraddhā*

Shraddhā is a disposition (overtly, an attitude) to keep acting regardless of the obstacles or the results. It is the focused movement of the awareness energy resulting in passionate commitment. In general, actions may be a

97

result of one's *tāmasic, rājasic* or *sāttvic* potential or some combination of the three. ***Tāmasic* action** is expressed through physical senses and is experienced as "physically, here-and- now." ***Rājasic* action** happens in time and space, and expresses as movement to sustain current experience by a combination of an attempt to control one's environment, and by deferring gratification of immediate physical experiences. ***Sāttvic* expression** is a movement in self-awareness, towards letting go of attachments of the *ahamkāra*, with physical space and time bound experiences. It should be noted here that the goal of this process of analyzing and labeling actions, which may seem like an overelaborate exercise of mere categorization, is to strengthen and refine *sākshi*, the observer, rather than the *ahamkāra* with attachments, the player in the game of life. The *sāttvic* dimension of each type of action is considered to be the best jumping-off point for activating *buddhi*, but all three *gunās* are always in play in our lives. To clearly understand how we operate as human beings, we need to understand how the three potentials manifest in various types of actions.

Developing a framework and a set of categories to help us examine our daily actions is essential to the Advaita Life Coaching process.

> *The challenge is not to eradicate one or the other of the action types or guṇā patterns but to keep them in a balance that constantly changes in relation to our inner needs and the world around us, as we move through life.*

In this essay, we will apply the terminology of the three *gunās* potentials to the four types of daily actions and develop guidelines to help us with our introspection.

The Four Types of Actions

The four types of action are

- *Āhārā:* grasping and consuming

- *Yagnyā*: setting up of the action environment, performance of daily routines and specific activities in our field of actions

- *Tapasyā*: deferring immediate gratification with focused action, to obtain fruits in the future

- *Dāna*: giving away fruits achieved through *yagnyā* and *tapasyā*

Āhārā: How We Act to Grasp and Consume

The first type of action, *āhārā,* is something that we perform almost all the time. We grasp and consume the air we breathe. We grasp and consume the food we eat, the water we drink. We grasp and consume videos on TV and the Internet. We grasp and consume when we read from a book, magazine or a newspaper. We regurgitate and consume our memories over and over again.

To keep the human body functioning, it requires a minimum amount of consumption. Consuming air, food and water are basic *tāmasic* activities, since they support the continued use of the physical senses. When we grasp-and-consume exercise, academic studies, preparation of a business plan, and even opportunities for *sāttvic* step-back and observation, these activities are considered *rājasic*. Some *tāmasic* consumption, a degree of satisfaction of the physical senses is necessary for survival as are some levels of *rājasic* consumption - deploying and deferring action in time and space - and of *sāttvic* consumption, if only as a resting point.

The challenge is not to eradicate one or the other of these action types or *gunā* patterns but to keep them in a balance that constantly changes in relation to our inner needs and the world around us, as we move through life. For instance, as we highlighted in the fourth essay, and it bears repeating here, the *tāmasic* aspect (which *rajas*-driven westerners tend to feel is "bad") is a necessary pattern given the physicality of the human manifestation. Having water when thirsty or taking a daily nap is *tāmasic*. Having a massage for relaxation and healing is *tāmasic*. But, so is having several bottles of wine or becoming a "massage junkie." One type of activity helps balance, the other triggers imbalance. It is not the *tāmasic* aspect of our being, *per se*, that is reduced in the course of the ALC practice; such reduction, if necessary, is an outgrowth of finding the required balance between *tāmasic*, *rājasic* and *sāttvic* tendencies, given contextual life cycle situations for each one of us.

Tāmasic Consumption

As mentioned in the earlier paragraph, all *āhārā* actions that involve physical sensation are in, some sense, *tāmasic*: we must eat, drink water and move away from pain and towards pleasure for our bodies to survive. What is true about consuming foods applies to consuming information, whether visual or auditory or tactile, as well. A certain level of consumption is required for physical sustenance and evokes the *tāmasic* pattern.

> *In the ALC process, we see questions as opportunities for observation, not as moralistic issues, only to become keenly aware of a pattern of behavior to discern if, and when, to change it.*

Similarly, learning to cook or selecting a mix of basic foods required to consume a healthy meal, and choosing to consume a form of entertainment like reading or listening to the news, may be required for basic health on a daily basis. However, an excess consumption of media and entertainment leads to blockage, just like an excessive consumption of food or drink.

Most of us give our *tāmasic āhārā* activities moral overtones and constant attention to our patterns of consumption: Are we eating too much? Drinking too much? Getting enough sun? Getting too much sun? Are we having too little sex or too much sex? And, so on. In the ALC process, we see these questions as opportunities for observation, not moralistic issues; the repeated questioning, for instance, of a particular type of consumption – if it is for immediate gratification without regard for balance – is only to become keenly aware of a pattern of behavior to discern if, and when, to change it.

Through guided inquiry and observation, rather than through willful force or helpless passivity, we can begin to take the first step toward bringing our experience of physical sensations into balance. In other words, to return to the metaphor of the two birds on the tree, we do not seek to eliminate the eating bird that is grasping and consuming but to learn to observe him, from the point of view of the watching bird. This is a process, not a one-shot analysis, and it takes time and training to do it effectively. Over time, the observer bird becomes dominant and the eating bird plays a minimal role required by the physical space-time aspect of the human manifestation.

Rājasic Consumption

In the Western culture, the kind of grasping action manifested through the *gunā* pattern known as *rājasic* is also very prevalent and often given a positive moral valuation. When we grasp at a diet plan or exercise program to increase muscle-mass and improve BMI-ratio, to run the marathon or for a longer life, we are delaying immediate gratification of the senses and working with our experience in space and time to achieve a goal. At ALC we categorize such activities as *rājasic* pattern. Practice of such patterns of consumption help to move us away from excessive *tāmasic* patterns, while helping maintain physical health, a key foundation for emotional and intellectual health. On the other hand, an indulgence in *rājasic* patterns, for example, to change one's body type through extreme exercise and diet to fit a socially acceptable model, becomes a hindrance to activate and sustain *sāttvic* patterns.

> *ALC processes do not prescribe specific levels or types of 'tāmasic' or 'rājasic' consumption that may be beneficial. What it supports is the creation of an individualized, regular practice to increase and maintain the self-awareness 'sāttvic' potential*

Sāttvic Consumption

Most of us who operate in western cultural modes have weak *sāttvic* or the peaceful, self-awareness potential, necessary to balance the other *gunās* of *tamas* and *rajas*. ALC processes do not prescribe a specific level or type of *tāmasic* or *rājasic* consumption or non-consumption that may be beneficial. What it does support is the creation of an individualized, regular practice to increase and maintain the self-awareness *sāttvic* potential so that you learn to discern, without effort, what to consume and how much.

The level of *sāttvic* awareness you want to reach will depend upon the depth of your practice. For instance, you may begin to recognize that certain kinds of foods, like alcohol or coffee consumed beyond a certain amount, or the hyper-way in which you are pursuing long-term goals or how you are controlling your environment, seriously curtails your ability to become aware or maintain self-awareness. ALC will support you as you make your choices accordingly.

The prerequisites to activate and sustain a **rājasic pattern** are: stable physical health (which requires that you consume the minimum required), and a desire to achieve a degree of control over one's future well-being (through repeated *rājasic* actions over time.) The prerequisite for activating and sustaining *sāttvic* patterns are: a level of emotional and intellectual maturity reached through success in sustaining and maintaining *rājasic* patterns, and self-awareness, and an understanding that *rājasic* actions do not lead to real control or even minimize the uncertainty of physical experiences. Rather than eradicating problems in the *tāmasic* domain, ALC helps strengthen *rājasic and sāttvic* manifestations.

Yagnyā: How We Act to Create Environments for Our Lives

The second action type we will consider is that of *Yagnyā*. ALC interprets this type of action as a modality that allows us to cleanse and set up our

> Just as the sun's rays, when focused through a convex lens, produce enough heat to set fire to a piece of paper, so also focused intellectual and emotional effort bursts into great musical compositions, writings, inventions, discoveries, political and social movements.

environment for daily routines and for specific events. It makes use of the metabolic fire/energy/heat created within the body through *āhārā* or consumption of food and information.

The individual with a preponderance of the *tāmasic* potential will do *yagnyā* to set up an attractive ambience for pleasurable activities like social parties, dancing, performances and sexual expression. A successful **tāmasic yagnyā** will provide a platform for satisfying immediate sensations through the physical senses; a home will be well appointed with the best furniture, audio and video entertainment, a pool table, a well-stocked bar, and so on.

Rājasic yagnyā develops and provides platforms for hard work with expected results in future pleasures. Setting up a work environment, including business process and infrastructure, and training people to work productively in such an environment, is an example of such *yagnyā*. Effective study habits and setting up space and time for study towards success in tests leading to admissions or jobs are also examples of *rājasic yagnyā*.

Sāttvic yagnyā provides a platform for increased and continual self-awareness at physical, emotional and intellectual level with a balance of physical and breath exercises, study, contemplation, and meditation. While ashrams and monasteries are examples of *sāttvic yagnyā*, an individual's home can be transformed once a week for a few hours or, in many instances, as an ongoing *sāttvic* platform.

Tapasyā: How We Act to be Productive

Tapasyā, the third of the four action types we examine in this essay, is focused and sustained effort, whether physical, emotional or intellectual. It has an *āhāric* dimension and it is undertaken on the *yagnyā* platform we create. Just as the sun's rays, when focused through a convex lens, produce enough heat to set fire to a piece of paper, so also focused intellectual and emotional effort bursts into great musical compositions, writings, inventions, discoveries, political and social movements.

At an individual level, **tāmasic tapasyā** may come about through focused study of immediate pleasure giving activities. Study of wines and wine tasting, which gives immediate pleasure, is one such example. Spending time on dressing and make up in front of mirror, and priming one's physical beauty, is another example.

Rājasic tapasyā defers pleasure and uses actions extended over time and space to lay the groundwork for future pleasurable material results. The typical seven year-long medical education program followed by multi-year residencies is an example of *rājasic tapasyā*. It is, in most cases, a precondition for material results but one should also note that it depends on ongoing *āhārā* or consuming and *yagnyā*, and that the goals of such *tapasyā* can never be certain.

Sāttvic tapasyā is focused and sustained effort in long-term daily physical and breath exercises, contemplation and meditation. It, too, has an *āhāric* dimension - if only a consumption of breath and seed sounds - and a *yajnic* dimension of platform-building, to create an environment that allows continual expression of focused actions that leads to deeper understanding of one's own nature and of the universe of experiences. *Sāttvic tapasyā* leads to more effective use of energies towards *rājasic* and *tāmasic* actions, as the triggers for material desires, current or in the future, begin to occur less often and more efficiently.

Dāna: How We Act to Give Away the Results of Our Actions

The fourth and last action-type we examine is *Dāna*, the renouncing or giving away some of the fruits obtained through *āhārā, yagnyā* and *tapasyā*. This activity is a challenge to the 'I'-ness, the *ahamkāra*, which attaches itself to memories of pleasures and the material objects that provide such

> *The question to ask is whether the action of giving is in exchange for something, immediate or future, or if it is to help free us from attachments.*

pleasure. The question to ask when examining the *dāna* action is whether the action of giving is in exchange for some immediate or future results, or if it will help free us from attachments. The answer to that question gives us clues to whether the giving is of the *tāmasic, rājasic* or *sāttvic* type.

Tāmasic dāna, giving for immediate pleasures, is exemplified by people who give excessively large tips at bars and hotels in return for personalized attention and services that may not be generally available. Such giving is tied directly to expectation of sense pleasures. It whets the appetite rather than reducing desires.

Examples of *rājasic dāna* abound in the world of modern billionaire-philanthropy. Giving is, partly, for the value of tax deductions and, partly, for social status and/or pushing the implementation of personal agendas. The desire for power and influence is fueled by such giving, adding to the material attachments the *ahamkāra*, the 'I' ness, may have.

Sāttvic dāna is giving to decrease attachments. Giving up sugar for weight loss may be rājasic if the goal is to have a more presentable body for better social acceptance. Fasting one day in a month to give up one's meal to a soup kitchen, as part of a process to observe and understand how the sensual urge to grasp works so that it can be restrained, is one example of *sāttvic dāna.* Such type of activities helps to deepen self-awareness and loosen the *ahamkāra* attachments. Deep groundwork in *sāttvic yagnyā* and *tapasyā* is required before true *sāttvic dāna* can take place; as desires begin to calm down, attachments loosen and giving away comes easily.

In sum, *sāttvic yagnyā* and *tapasyā* leads to *dāna* resulting in a simpler external life, a reflection of the inner calm. As we've said before, such inner calm is a by-product, not the goal, of this process. The goal is simply to strengthen the role of the *buddhi* with its self-aware observer capacity.

SEVEN

TYĀGA: MAKING GIVING AWAY FREELY PART OF YOUR ACT

Based on Chapter Eighteen of the Bhagavad Gita

Tyāga, Giving Away | Role of Gunās in Tyāga. | The Dynamic Driving Tyāga | Tyāga in the Twenty-First Century.

In the previous essay we talked about the four action-types we perform: *āhārā, yagnyā, tapasyā* and *dāna*. Each supports all of the *tāmasic, rājasic* and *sāttvic* potentials.

For instance, whatever we consume through *āhārā*, or grasping actions, can nourish

> *The act of complete giving is called 'Tyāga,' and it is possible only when the 'ahamkāra' lets go of all attachments to actions and the fruits of actions it has accumulated through 'āhārā,' 'yagnyā' and 'tapasyā.'*

immediate pleasure (*tāmasic*), delay gratification (*rājasic*), or increase self-awareness (*sāttvic*).

Likewise, depending on how we channel what we consume, or the environment or platform we create for it, *yagnyā* can be *tāmasic, rājasic* or *sāttvic*. Our focused actions of *yagnyā* and *tapasyā*, in both the *tāmasic* and *rājasic* mode, gies results that only sustain the grasping and consuming cycle; *dāna* or giving away accomplished by activating these potentials does not make you more self-aware. On the other hand, the action of *dāna* when done through the activation of the *sāttvic* potential increases the role of *buddhi* in our lives; the quality of self-awareness and discrimination increases to sustain a balance in our work, relationships and money spaces.

In this essay, based on the Chapter Eighteen of the Gita, we see how *dāna,* partial giving, is taken one step further to the act of complete giving, called **Tyāga**. The act of complete giving is possible only when the *ahamkāra* lets go of all attachments to actions and the fruits of actions it has accumulated through *aahara, yagnyā* and *tapasyā*. This new term and its meaning help us distinguish between a) "giving for the sake of getting" and the accompanying cycle of grasping-consumption; and b) moving to a plane of action and expression where we continually give, and make ourselves vulnerable by not expecting or grasping for anything in return. As we have frequently noted, none of the actions are inherently "good" or "bad" but only prevent or accelerate deepening of the self-awareness and observation. *Sāttvic dāna* is one step on the way to self-awareness, whereas *tyāga* is a qualitative change.

We all give up or give away many things for different reasons. For example, some of us give up a hard college course for an easy one, knowing that the harder one could

> *'Tyāga' moves us to a plane of action and expression where we continually give, and make ourselves vulnerable by not expecting or grasping for anything in return.*

potentially propel us further along, because the teacher grades strictly or it requires a lot of work leaving no time for socializing, and so on. Working less hard to satisfy immediate desires is **tāmasic tyāga** because our goal is immediate pleasure or ease of life.

Then, there is a group of students who take a heavy course load and study into the night and over weekends in the library, giving up fun today so that they can get into medical school in a few years. They know that, by giving up certain kinds of pleasure in the present, they will potentially have more material gain in the future. Such types of students are the *rājasic tyāgis* because they give up immediate gratification for future gains. They will likely end up being captains of industry, leaders in medicine and CEOs of hedge funds. Their future gains could cause pain to others, but the depth of their *tyāga* increases the probability of achieving desirable material goals in the future.

> *An example of 'sāttvic tyāga' might be tutoring a child or adult for free, making a meal for or visiting with the elderly. The key is to not talk about your experiment with anyone; the less the better and, with no one, to make it an ideal practice.*

And, where there are *tāmasic* and *rājasic tyāgas*, there must be *sāttvic tyāgas*, as well. This is how this universe of experiences is roped together, always intertwined and twisted together by the three strong threads of these potentials. Ever so often we may come across students who are willing and able to help others. They do this not to pad their resumes or for favors in exchange (examples of *rājasic tyāga*), but simply because they have something to give that others truly need. Such students or members of one's community are really hard to spot, because they do not toot their horns (that would instantly make their *tyāga* or action of giving away *rājasic* in nature.)

How would you know what *sāttvic tyāga* really looks like? You could start by experimenting for yourself. Your ALC Coach will work with you to develop a practice that begins by taking between ten minutes per day and up to one hour per week. During this time you will do something for another just for the joy of doing it, without expecting or, even more importantly, wanting anything in return including, if possible, associating your name with the giving. To practice *tyāga*, we need to cultivate a good deal of *sāttvic dāna* to arouse the *buddhi* because it is often hard to discern if we can and are willing give away our time, knowledge and energy for no apparent returns. An example of our expression of *sāttvic tyāga* might be tutoring a child or adult for free, making a meal for or visiting with the elderly. Just do it, as someone has said, and see what happens to your own personality. The key is to not talk about your experiment with anyone; the less said the better and, with no one, to make it an ideal practice.

In the ALC process, we suggest several *sāttvic tyāga* experiments and let you determine what works best for you. By the very nature of the experiments, there is no designing or monitoring. The ALC approach not only focuses on helping you understand the nature of *tāmasic, rājasic* and *sāttvic tyāga* but also provides direction on how you can move from *tāmasic* to *rājasic* and, then, to *sāttvic tyāga*.

What Drives *Tyāga*, the Dynamic of Giving Away?

To help us better draw on the dynamic of giving away or *tyāga*, Chapter Eighteen of the Bhagavad Gita also discusses its precursor: the dynamic of action which is being given up in *tyāga*. Action in the human manifestation is seen to be a dynamic between knowledge, the knower, and the object of the knowledge.

An example will help us understand the notion of action: I am thirsty and see a glass of water, and I know that drinking the water will

> Attachments of the 'ahamkāra' begin to be expressed as identity... The more we spin the web of identity, the more we accumulate in the 'potential to give away' column, and the more 'tyāga' work we have to do.

quench my thirst. In this case, the sensing of thirst is the "knower," the specific information that water will quench thirst is "knowledge," and the perceived glass of water is "object of the knowledge." Action results from the dynamic between the *ahamkāra* (the thirst sensing-grasping) and the glass of water being consumed, due to the intermediation of the knowledge that "consuming water will quench thirst." The need for *tyāga* arises when the action is triggered due to habituation or attachment. Let's replace the glass of water with the addict's glass of vodka and work through the dynamic of action "to quench thirst." Here, the need for repeated ingestion of vodka is no longer thirst-quenching but is habitual. The habitual action takes away awareness from what is required for continued well-being of the individual. Another example is the need to travel to work which triggers the need for a car. If, as a response to this need, you purchase a high-end luxury car which not only transports you but also increases your status among friends, family and colleagues, your attachment to the car goes beyond the basic need for transport.

Such attachments of the *ahamkāra* begin to be expressed as identity: I am a doctor, lawyer, engineer etc; I am successful; I am rich. The more we spin the web of identity, the more we accumulate in the 'potential to give away' column and the more *tyāga* work we have to do. What attachments and habits should we have to give up, and in what sequence and timing? Again, ALC is not prescriptive in its approach, and only provides a process so that the realizations of what needs to be given up and when arise out of the individual contemplative-meditative practices.

The human manifestation acts through its physical senses in the here-and-now, while it acts through its subtle body in space and time. Once it manifests itself fully through its actions without forming attachments, it has energies available for exploration of its own nature and the nature of the universe of experiences. If the individual in the process of acting becomes attached to the actions, its energies are diverted and drained towards maintaining such actions.

For instance, the attachment or habituation could be to excessive sleep and physical relaxation. Giving up exercise or work in an apparent effort to free up one's energy for subtle *sāttvic* work is counter-productive. Excessive sleeping is an activity diverting energy into the actual practice of being lazy, the latter in itself an activity to which we can also get habituated.

The sum of the discussion here is that it is not the *gunā* of the action that ultimately matters, or the nature of the action itself. What truly matters is the *tyāga*, the giving up or the renouncing of attachments and expectations of results from our actions. Only this full renunciation can help us move away from habitual actions towards becoming a spontaneous and consistent subtle striver, looking for maximum awareness and openness in every minute. It is not about giving up of current pleasures for future gains, which would be *rājasic dāna*. It is also not about giving up current actions that would lead to future gains only because they are too difficult, which would be *tāmasic dāna*. It is not even, in a true subtle striver, the giving up of other activities to achieve self-awareness, which would be *sāttvic dāna*. *Tyāga* is beyond all three.

Tyāga in the Twenty-First Century

In the twentieth-century and in the first decade of the current one, the key growth factors in the economy were productive

> *A culture that encourages delayed gratification also implicitly discourages some manifestations of 'tamas' -- seeking and consuming immediate pleasure is not acceptable. On the other hand, it actively encourages 'rājasic' attachments to social status and wealth.*

investment and personal consumption. Productive investment was made by saving on current income by decreasing current consumption, investing in activities leading to future results and, therefore, future consumption. The motivational drivers in this period were (and are, even today) *rājasic* in nature. Delayed gratification, through austerity measures, was considered the hallmark of a growing economy; even today, austerity is encouraged so that we will have more money to consume in the future.

A culture that encourages delayed gratification also implicitly discourages some manifestations of *tamas* - seeking and consuming immediate pleasure is not acceptable. On the other hand, it actively encourages *rājasic* attachments to social status and wealth: those who rent should want to buy their first home; those who live in a small house should want a bigger house, or a vacation home, and even more. If they are millionaires, they should want to become billionaires. Almost everyone is seduced and convinced to get onto the treadmill of *rājasic* activities.

The challenge in the long-term, when current social norms drive us to minimize *tamas* and maximize our *rajas*, is to hold both these potentials at the minimum levels while maximizing our *sāttvic* potential.

The *tyāga* practice then is a two-step process:

- The first step focuses on our *rājasic* actions of delayed physical gratification to gain material wellbeing. Such a shift in focus teaches us to utilize our energy fully to navigate space-time in the face of its uncertainties.

- The second step focuses on our *sāttvic* actions to achieve awareness, putting attention on understanding one's own nature and the nature of the universe of experiences. Such a shift in focus teaches us to act without expecting or attaching to any results, other than the minimal required to sustain the physical human manifestation, and frees our energy fully to be a subtle striver

What *Tyāga* is Right for You?

The physical, emotional and intellectual maturity level reached at a particular point in time, and in the context of the specific attachments formed with family, friends and social institutions, determines where you should begin with *tyāga*. Accelerating the *tyāga* process beyond what might be appropriate leads to imbalance for individuals and for those around them. Many of us know people who have tried grand gestures of renunciation which have destabilized both their own physical, mental and spiritual health, and the lives of those closely associated with them.

Discerning the right level of *tyāga* is one of the most important things an Advaita Life Coach can do for you. For instance, a few twenty-year olds who are emotionally and intellectually mature, physically strong, and not committed to personal attachments of family, may be ready for *tyāga* and to move from *rājasic* to *sāttvic* activities. The rest may have to go through a few more decades of *rājasic* activities before they can focus on *sāttvic* activities. But even this group, if they become aware of the dynamic of *tamas-rajas-sattva* and where it could potentially lead them, can act on the stage of the *rājasic* theater in a manner where their role gradually becomes more and more *sāttvic*. Living simply while delaying attachments to material things, even while raising a family for example, may position them such that, by time they are fifty years old, they can focus more and more on the *sāttvic,* and less and less on the *rājasic* expression of *tyāga.*

ALC is sensitive to the life-cycle context of each individual when designing a coaching program. It helps to determine where you are currently in the *tamas-rajas-sattva* dimensions, and what makes sense in how quickly you want to begin changing the current configuration. For example, if you are a thirty-five year old career-oriented professional and mother of two young children, and feeling overwhelmed, you can explore the ALC process as a way of balancing your current life-style. Depending on where you are in the *tamas-rajas-sattva* configuration, the ALC process will begin with a method of contemplation to help you understand the bigger picture of your situation and the tradeoffs within your *rajas* activities, to make them more manageable and fruitful, while ensuring physical, emotional, intellectual and spiritual health. Coaching is tailored to stabilize the *rājasic* and monitor progress over time, to decide when and how to progress towards more *sāttvic* activities.

We discussed in the first essay how the current globalizing culture, with its roots in European Enlightenment, is driven by the *rājasic* paradigm: work hard, delay material gratification, accumulate more and more potential material gratification (dollar net-worth), and then enjoy by consuming such accumulated gratification credits. Based on extensive research into economics, business and psychology in the twentieth century, methods to carry out this *rājasic* mission efficiently and effectively have been developed. ALC acknowledges and incorporates some of these methods within its tool set. It is especially helpful for those who are at a point where they need to minimize *tāmasic* actions and move towards successful *rājasic* actions – from actions leading to instant, immediate gratification to consistent focused actions with delayed gratification. It also helps those who want to stabilize their *rājasic* actions by making them more efficient and effective so that they have more resources, including time, to focus on *sāttvic* actions. The twentieth century methods used in the ALC framework include time-based planning and approaches to identify and pro-actively resolve potential problems to manage risks and decrease uncertainties in material life. The further goal, however, is to take small, organized, guided steps through real-time concrete practices and suggestions, in parallel, to increase the intensity of *sāttvic* actions in the mix.

| EIGHT |

TOWARDS BECOMING SAKSHI:
THE OBSERVER

Based on Chapter Fifteen of the Bhagavad Gita

Bringing it all Together | Foundational Work
The Advaita Life Coaching Starting Point

The essays in this collection have focused on Chapters Thirteen to Eighteen of the Bhagavad Gita, with particular attention paid to Chapter Four (Yoga of Knowledge) that is incorporated into in the third essay. We now turn to Chapter Fifteen of the Bhagavad Gita which states the end goal for the concepts and categories we have been

> *Our experiences, which are ever changing, are manifestations of the 'One that is Unchanging;' that each one of us is a manifestation of that which is changeless, and what we are about to consume and digest is also a manifestation of that oneness.*

laying out. This chapter of the Gita has a special significance to many communities in India: its twenty verses are chanted prior to starting the main meal of the day (typically the mid-day meal.) They serve as a powerful and succinct reminder that all our experiences, which are ever changing, are manifestations of the "One that is Unchanging;" that each one of us is a manifestation of that which is changeless, and what we are about to consume and digest is also a manifestation of that oneness, just like the vital energy that we experience in our physical body is the manifestation of that same changeless one.

As a reminder to my readers: the Bhagavad Gita is framed by the story of the epic *Mahabharata* War. The war, which takes place between two sides of the same family, can also be understood as a fight between those who want to become subtle strivers and those who want to excel as material experiencers. The role of the narrator of the Gita is to observe and record, in "real-time," the question and answers between the leader of the subtle strivers, Arjuna, and his charioteer, the one that is the unchanging universal energy, represented by Sri Krishna, against the backdrop of the imminent war on the battlefield. This question-and-answer format allows Sri Krishna to explain abstract *Advaita* concepts to non-philosophers. In all but one chapter of the Gita, the questions Arjuna raises are pointed: What is the responsibility of the subtle striver when overcoming opposition from material experiencers?

From the ALC perspective, the conflict that takes place between the *sādhakā* subtle striver and the *samsarika* material experiencer within us is not so much an issue of managing the supposed struggle but more about finding a balance between the two, at various points, in our life cycle.

The Fifteenth Chapter is significantly different in that Arjuna poses no question that initiates the response from Sri Krishna. The narrator relays Sri Krishna's words to us, starting

When do we begin to get a sense of our true nature?

directly with a metaphorical description of the universe of experiences, rapidly focusing on how universal energy is active in all experiences, and how the awareness aspect of the human manifestation can realize its true nature.

In practical terms, with our set of practices as our drivers, our actions move from being a mix of *tāmasic* and *rājasic* to becoming mostly *rājasic* and, subsequently, focusing on becoming increasingly *sāttvic*. In such movement, we begin to get a sense of the true nature of ourselves as an expression of the universal energy. How?

The first step is becoming an observer of our actions (through our *karmendriyas*) and to understand the impact of our actions as experiences (through our *jnanendriyas*.) To be an observer implies we do not have attachment to either our actions or our experiences. In turn, that means that we do not ascribe a positive (good) or negative (bad) quality to our experiences and our actions. A byproduct of movement to becoming an observer is that we do not react to our experiences and we act only to maintain our balance. For example, if someone says to me I am

> *Our interpretation of our experiences is limited by the capabilities of our cognitive tools of 'manas,' 'chitta,' 'buddhi' and 'ahamkāra.' Is there a way of extending or fully utilizing our limited capabilities?*

stupid or that I do not deserve something, I should not react to such statements. Such non-reaction is only possible if I am firmly grounded in not having my identity shaped by what others think of me, and if I feel I am dependent on consuming certain experiences which 'I deserve.'

Sākshi: The Journey of the Subtle Striver

We move, as *Sādhakās* or subtle strivers, towards becoming the Observer, *Sākshi.* In this movement we begin realizing the limitations of our action capabilities, *karmendriyas*. And our interpretation of our experiences is limited by the capabilities of our cognitive tools of *manas, chitta, buddhi* and *ahamkāra.* Is there a way of extending or fully utilizing our limited capabilities? This collection of essays so far identified specific capability-building practices of *shraddhā, yagnyā, tapasyā, dāna* and *tyāga*, facilitated by physical well-being, breath-work, contemplation and meditation. Becoming *Sākshi* the Observer, is a state of mind that can be sustained after considerable practice of focused concentrated actions, passionate commitment, and letting go of specific attachments.

The Foundational Work and the ALC Starting Point

With the foundational work of *shraddhā, tapasyā* and *tyāga* in place, the process of becoming a subtle striver starts with the contemplation of our social identity. Such a social identity is an aggregation of the roles we play in the work, relational and money life spaces in the twenty-first century, with the concomitant expectations and fears about the future. We, thus, return to where we started in the first essay: to achieve a balance in these life spaces, we need to begin shifting away from being material experiencers towards becoming subtle strivers. It is the subtle striver who moves to becoming the *Sākshi*, the Observer, which Chapter Fifteen of the Bhagavad Gita points to.

The shift from an attachment-laden *ahamkāra* of a material experiencer towards a mostly detached subtle striver *ahamkāra* is a dynamic that requires sustained practice. The velocity of the movement depends on where we are located in the web of our attachments when we initiate our practice. The ALC process begins at this point, helping to identify the location of our *ahamkāra* in our web of attachments.

| NINE |

THE ADVAITA LIFE COACHING PROCESS

Synthesis of Advaita Approach with Twenty-First Century Tools

How Advaita Life Coaching Works

The Advaita Life Coaching process combines concepts and tools from the Indian *Advaita* traditions and twenty-first century American planning and strategy methods. The process starts with you, when you take the small step to

> *When you decide to explore ALC coaching further, you will begin to develop an integrated view of your own path of balance between and among professional, relational and money spaces.*

articulate, by responding to a brief questionnaire, how balanced you perceive you are in the work, relationship and money spaces – the three theaters in which you play roles

The ALC coach assesses your responses in terms of where you may be located in the *tamas-rajas-sattva* framework and where the perceived imbalances may exist, between the roles you play, in the professional, relational and financial theaters. As part of the assessment, the ALC coach provides a reflection with a view to help you become more aware of what a balance between the roles in the three theaters may look like.

When you decide to explore ALC coaching further, you will begin to develop an integrated view of your own path of balance between and among professional, relational and money spaces. Your coach will help you become aware of how the roles you play are being enabled by your *sāttvic, rājasic* and *tāmasic* potentials, and how you can re-prioritize and refine the roles to improve your balance and efficiency. Eventually, you will learn to monitor these by yourself.

From then on, you generate the dynamic by which to bring your *gunās* into balance, a dynamic that constantly changes as your awareness of your roles and theaters of action change. Your coach will help you refine your awareness through an ever-more subtle and precise sense of the categories and concepts we have been introducing in this essay series: *āhārā, yagnyā, tapasyā,* and *dāna.* Your coach will work with you to clarify your current priorities to suggest a set of tailored contemplative practices designed to help you focus better and create the momentum you seek to move toward your goals.

Along the way, the ALC coach will support your disciplined actions and, in parallel as you begin to see results, may suggest refinements on the execution of your plan.

This process, when followed with *shraddhā* passionate commitment, has the potential of bringing about a deep sea change in your life, including more effective and less stressful actions, and greater self-awareness and peace of mind. As you move toward *dāna* and begin to be empowered to perform it by your own new effectiveness in dealing with the world, you will have laid a strong and enduring framework and developed and effective practice for becoming a *sādhakā,* a subtle striver toward the formation of a mature *ahamkāra* and the activation of the deep power of *buddhi*.

You may at any point, of course, take the gains you have made and "cash in" on the clarity and momentum you have gained. You can do this before the *dāna* actions, or you can go back to the beginning and repeat the steps again. Even if you do stop at an early point in the ALC process, you will still experience results on the material plane, and there is nothing wrong with this. But if you are serious about stepping fully in to the subtle striver role, the tools that the ALC process will provide will still be essential to helping you define and stabilize your ground.

GLOSSARY

The explanations provided below describe my interpretation of the Sanskrit words used in the essays.

Sanskrit	**Interpretation**
Āhāra	That which is consumed by the physical body.
Ādi Shankara	Paraphrased from Wikipedia: Ādi Śaṅkara, pronounced [aːdʑ ɕəŋkərə]) (788 CE - 820 CE), also known as Śaṅkara Bhagavatpādācārya and Ādi Śaṅkarācārya, was an Indian sage from Kalady in present-day Kerala who consolidated the doctrine of *advaita vedānta*.[1][2] His teachings are based on the unity of the *ātman* and *brahman*— non-dual brahman, in which brahman is viewed as *nirgunā* brahman, brahman without attributes.
Advaitā	A-Dvaita, Non-Dual, refers to a school of thought which propounds that the human potential for self-awareness arises out of undifferentiated universal energy,

Brahman. Realization of such non-duality requires rigorous training and practice and leads the individual to lead a balanced life of non-attachment in harmony with his or her experiences.

Aham   The 'I am' vibration that we experience when we focus on being aware of our being

Ahamkarā   That which vibrates as *Aham*

Apāna   One of five vital energies in the human manifestation that helps with elimination of all that which the physical and subtle body does not require for its nourishment.

Arjunā   Paraphrased from Wikipedia: In the epic **Mahabharata**, Arjuna plays one of the most important roles as the dear friend and brother-in-law of Lord Krishna, who acted as his charioteer on the battlefield of **Kurukshetra**, and from whom he heard the **Bhagavad Gita** before the

	start of the war.
Asurās	Material Experiencers
Āsuric	The quality of focusing on material experience.
Ātmā Bodhā	A treatise on knowledge of the self by **Adi Shankarā**
Ātman	
Avadhūta Gitā	"Song of the Ascetic" expounding concepts of *Advaita*
Bhagavad Gitā	A 700-verse poem that is part of the ancient Sanskrit epic Mahabharata. Scholars roughly date the Bhagavad Gita to the period between 200 BCE and 200 CE, the Gita having been influenced by the constructs of *Sankhya* philosophical tradition and the *Upanishads*.
Brahman	Undifferentiated universal energy which is the continual source of all manifested experiences, including space-time and matter, as well as experiencers which are an extension of space-time and matter.

Buddhi	It is that aspect of the human manifestation which has the capacity to be aware of human experiences as well as the experiencer, the *Ahamkāra*.
Chitta	Aspect of the human manifestation that stores data of physical experiences and space-time causative perceptions of those experiences.
Dāna	The fourth step, of giving away part of the results obtained, in the four step human action cycle identified in the 17th chapter of the Bhagavad Gita, the first three being *Āhāra, Yagnyā* and *Tapasyā*.
Gunās	Potentials for experience which are an integral part of the five elements of earth, water, fire, air and space: *Tamas* - potential for physical experiences here and now; *Rajas* - potential for experiences in space-time; *Sattva* - potential to observe actions

	driven by *Tamas* and *Rajas*.
Indriyās	Cognitive and physical action functions
Jīva	Aspect of awareness capability of **Buddhi** that identifies itself as separate (**Ahamkāra**) and develops identification with **Rājasic** and **Tāmasic** experiences stored in **Chitta.**
Jñāna	Cognitive capability of the human manifestation.
Jñanendriyā	Cognitive action functions
Karma Yogin	An individual who steadfastly acts in a **Rājasic** manner and then gives away most of the fruits obtained from such actions, thus becoming aware of the process of detaching the **Ahamkāra** from the memories stored in the **Chitta.**
Karmendriyā	Physical action functions
Kshetra	Field of Activity for an individual
Kshetrayagnyā	The individual acting in a **Kshetra**
Kurukshetra	Field of activity of the **Kuru** clan in

the *Mahabharata*

Leela	Theater, as in 'Life-is-a-Stage on which we perform.'
Manas	Aspect of the human manifestation in which thoughts are formed through interaction of physical experiences with inputs from *Chitta* and *Ahamkāra*.
Nirgunā	Without form, potential for or attributes of experiences.
Nirvanā Shatakam	Adi Shankara's six verses on self-identification.
Māhābhāratā	A Sanskrit epic, earliest known textual form from the 4th century BCE based on narrations from at least 9th century BCE.
Patanjali's Yoga Sutrās	The Yoga Sūtras of Patañjali are 196 sūtras (aphorisms) that constitute the foundational text of *Sankhya Yoga*.
Prakriti	Active creative manifestation of *Brahman*, the undifferentiated one source of all experiential manifestations.

Prāna	The overarching of the five vital energies, which integrates space-time with physical experiences with cognitive and action functions.
Purushā	Observer manifestation of **Brahman**, the undifferentiated one source of all experiential manifestations.
Rājasic	One of three **Gunās**, potential for experiences in space-time.
Sādhakā	Subtle striver
Sādhanā	The process of striving for the subtle.
Sākshi	Observer.
Samāna	One of four vital energies in the human manifestation used for digestion of *Āhāra*.
Samsārikā	Material Experiencer
Sānkhya	'Counting'; also used to label an Indian philosophical tradition that enumerates the breakdown of the one to specific numbers of experience and experiencer manifestations.
Sāttvic	One of three **Gunās**, potential for

experiencing as an observer.

Shraddhā	Passionate focused commitment
Sūkshmā	Subtle
Tāmasic	One of three *Gunās,* potential for physical experience here and now.
Tapasyā	Focused action over extended period of time until desired results are achieved.
Tyāga	Giving away all of the fruits obtained through actions, a state possible only through detaching of the *Ahamkāra* of all misidentifications with memories stored in *Chitta.*
Ūdāna	One of five vital energies in the human manifestation used for expression e.g. as speech.
Upanishad	Summary of contemplative thought based on the four major Vedas: Rig, Yajur, Sama and Atharva.
Vedantā	School of thought based on the Upanishads.
Vivekachudāmani	Adi Shankarā's five-hundred-and-

eight verse exposition describing development of *Vivekā*—the capacity of discrimination, a capability of *Buddhi* aspect of the human manifestation —as the central task in the spiritual life. Adi Shankarā qualified *Vivekā* as the crown jewel of human manifestation.

Vyāna One of five vital energies in the human manifestation, which controls muscles and balances the physical human body.

Yagnyā The second of four action types described in Chapter 17 of the Bhagavad Gita, which sets up the environment for focused action (*Tapsyā*) and sequentially follows *Āhāra*.

Yoga Vashistha Six-thousand verse exposition of *Advaita Vedantā*.

The Advaita Life Practice

BIBLIOGRAPHY

Aurobindo, Sri. *Essays on the Gita.* Sri Aurobindo Ashram Trust, 1972, All India Books, Pondicherry – 2.

_____ *Savitri, A Legend and a Symbol.* 1993, Sri Aurobindo Ashram Trust, Pondicherry.

Balagangadhara, S.N. *The Heathen In His Blindness....* 2005, Ajay Kumar Jain for Manohar Publishers & Distributors, 4753/23 Ansari Road, Daryaganj, New Delhi 110 002.

Bryant, Edwin F. *The Yoga Sutras of Patanjali: With Insights from the Traditional Commentators.* 2009, North Point Press, NY 10011

Chinmayananda, Swami. *The Holy Geeta: Commentary.* 1992, Central Chinmaya Mission Trust, Bombay 400072

_____ *Isavasya Upanishad; Commentary.* 1992, Central Chinmaya Mission Trust, Bombay 400072.

_____*Mundakopinshad: Commentary.* 1997, Central Chinmaya Mission Trust, Bombay 400072.

_____*Discourses on Kenopanishad.* 1952, Central Chinmaya Mission Trust, Sandeepany Sadhanalaya, Saki Vihar Road, Bombay 400 072

_____*Discourses on Taitriya Upanishad.* 1992, Central Chinmaya Mission Trust, Sanipany Sadhanalaya, Saki Vihar Road, PowaI, Bombay 400 072.

_____*Discourse on Mandukya Upanishad*. 1990, Central Chinmaya Mission Trust, Sandeepany Sadhanalaya, Powai Park Drive, Bombay 400 072.

_____*Discourses on Vivekachudamani*. 1985, Central Chinmaya Mission Trust, Sandeepany Sadhanalaya, Powai Park Drive, Bombay 400 072.

Heinberg, Richard. *The End of Growth*. 2011, New Society Publishers, P.O. Box 189, Gabriola Island, BC VOR 1X0, Canada.

Jackson, Tim. *Prosperity without Growth*. 2009, Earthscan Ltd, Dunstan House, 14a St Cross Street, London EC1N 8XA, UK.

Jnanananda, Bharati Sri. *The Essence of Yoga Vashistha*. 1982, V. Sadanand, Amata Books, 10 Kamaraj Building, 573 Mount Road, Chennai, 600 006, India.

Krishnananda, Swami. *The Brihadaranyaka Upanishad*. 1984. The Divine Life Trust Society, Shivanandanagar, U.P.

Mal, Kannoo, **Murthy**, S.R. & Co. *The Avadhuta Gita of Dattatreya: Translation*. 1920 Triplicane, Madras (copy of book was available in pdf format at:

http://www.mediafire.com/?lyfy22tjy5d in 2011).

Pandit, M.P.   *A Summary of the Savitri.* 1995, Dipti Publications, Sri Aurobindo Ashram, Pondicherry 605002.

_____   *Yoga in Savitri.* 1976, Dipti Publications, Sri Aurobindo Ashram, Pondicherry, India.

www.ingramcontent.com/pod-product-compliance
Lightning Source LLC
Chambersburg PA
CBHW070959040426
42443CB00007B/583